HISTORY OF BASEBALL FOR KIDS

Basic Knowledge of Baseball
with Some Fun Facts and Records

WILLIAM LAWSON

©**Copyright 2021 - All rights reserved.**

The content contained within this book may not be reproduced, duplicated or transmitted without direct written permission from the author or the publisher.

Under no circumstances will any blame or legal responsibility be held against the publisher, or author, for any damages, reparation, or monetary loss due to the information contained within this book, either directly or indirectly.

Legal Notice:

This book is copyright protected. It is only for personal use. You cannot amend, distribute, sell, use, quote or paraphrase any part, or the content within this book, without the consent of the author or publisher.

Disclaimer Notice:

Please note the information contained within this document is for educational and entertainment purposes only. All effort has been executed to present accurate, up to date, reliable, complete information. No warranties of any kind are declared or implied. Readers acknowledge that the author is not engaged in the rendering of legal, financial, medical or professional advice. The content within this book has been derived from various sources. Please consult a licensed professional before attempting any techniques outlined in this book.

By reading this document, the reader agrees that under no circumstances is the author responsible for any losses, direct or indirect, that are incurred as a result of the use of the information contained within this document, including, but not limited to, errors, omissions, or inaccuracies.

Table of Contents

Introduction 1

Chapter 1: What Is Baseball? 5

    Baseball Fielding Positions 7

    Rules of Baseball 25

    Summary 32

Chapter 2: When Was Baseball Invented? 34

    Baseball as We Know It 34

    The Major League 40

    Evolution of Baseball 49

    Summary 54

Chapter 3: The Best Players in Every Position 56

    Best Players 57

    Summary 65

Chapter 4: The 20 Best Teams of all Time 67

    #20. 2002 Oakland Athletics 68

    #19. 2001 Seattle Mariners 68

    #18. 2016 Chicago Cubs 69

    #17. 1972 Oakland Athletics 69

    #16. 2018 Boston Red Sox 69

    #15. 1989 Oakland Athletics 70

#14. 1969 New York Mets 70

#13. 1995 Atlanta Braves 70

#12. 2004 Boston Red Sox 70

#11. 1968 Detroit Tigers 71

#10. 1967 St. Louis Cardinals 71

#9. 1927 New York Yankees 71

#8. 1976 Cincinnati Reds 72

#7. 1984 Detroit Tigers 72

#6. 1986 New York Mets 72

#5. 1970 Baltimore Orioles 72

#4. 1975 Cincinnati Reds 73

#3. 1961 New York Yankees 73

#2. 1939 New York Yankees 73

#1. 1998 New York Yankees 74

Summary 74

Chapter 5: The Best Coaches and Managers of all Time 75

#30. Bucky Harris 76

#29. Billy Southworth 76

#28. Dusty Baker 77

#27. Billy Martin 77

#26. Cito Gaston 78

#25. Cap Anson 78

#24. Frank Selee 79

#23. Dick Williams 79

#22. Billy McKechnie 80

#21. Fred Clarke 80

#20. Jim Leyland 81

#19. Davey Johnson 81

#18. Al Lopez 82

#17. Terry Francona 82

#16. Leo Durocher 83

#15. Jim Mutrie 83

#14. Frank Chance 83

#13. Bruce Bochy 84

#12. Tommy Losorda 84

#11. Miller Huggins 85

#10. Water Alston 85

#9. Connie Mack 85

#8. Bobby Cox 86

#7. Earl Weaver 87

#6. Tony La Russa 87

#5. Joe Torre 87

#4. Sparky Anderson 88

- #3. Casey Stengel 88
- #2. John McGraw 89
- #1. Joe McCarthy 89
- Summary 90

Chapter 6: Best Records and Fun Facts 92
- Best Records 92
- Fun Facts 97
- Summary 104

Chapter 7: Baseball Around the World 105
- Central/South America 105
- Europe 106
- Asia 106
- Australia 107
- Africa 107
- Summary 107

Chapter 8: Major League Teams 108
- Teams 108
- Team Fields 110
- Summary 113

Chapter 9: Minor League Baseball 115
- What Is Minor League Baseball? 115
- Minor League Tiers 122

- Minor League Salaries 123
- MiLB Team Owners 124
- Minor League Teams 124
- Top 12 Minor League Players 133
- Summary 135

Chapter 10: World Series History 136
- Fifteen World Series Moments to Remember 136
- Summary 143

Chapter 11: Twenty-Five Best Baseball Movies 144
- #1. Bull Durham (1988) 144
- #2. A League of Their Own (1992) 145
- #3. The Pride of the Yankees (1942) 145
- #4. Field of Dreams (1989) 145
- #5. Eight Men Out (1988) 146
- #6. Moneyball (2011) 146
- #7. The Natural (1984) 147
- #8. The Sandlot (1993) 147
- #9. Major League (1989) 148
- #10. The Bad News Bears (1976) 148
- #11. Bang the Drum Slowly (1973) 148
- #12. The Bingo Long Traveling All-Stars and Motor Kings (1976) 148

 #13. The Rookie (2002) 149

 #14. Take Me Out To the Ball Game 149

 #15. Da*n Yankees (1958) 149

 #16. Sugar (2008) 149

 #17. Fear Strikes Out (1957) 150

 #18. 42 (2013) 150

 #19. Rookie of the Year (1993) 150

 #20. Angels in the Outfield (1994) 150

 #21. 61 (2001) 150

 #22. Cobb (1994) 151

 #23. For the Love of the Game (1999) 151

 #24. Fever Pitch (2005) 151

 #25. Million Dollar Arm (2014) 151

 Honorable Mentions 152

Conclusion 153

Discussion 158

References 168

just for you

A Free Gift For Our Readers
Please grab your FREE
Sports History Starter Guide for Kids
by clicking the link below!

Introduction

Did you know that the sport known as the "American pastime" is actually popular all over the world? What sport is that? Baseball. You probably have a friend or family member that watches the sport on television religiously. Maybe you know someone who plays it in your town or at your school; they might even be the talk of the town where you're from! Every time you're around someone who loves the sport, you probably hear them talking excitedly about it and you might have no idea what they're talking about. Why do they keep mentioning the Braves and the Red Sox? Why is your friend's dad spending so much money to take a trip to Wrigley Field? Maybe you watched your parents jump up and down in the living room during the World Series, or maybe your best friend's favorite thing to do is play catch in the backyard.

Baseball is something that I have always been passionate about. Whether I was playing it on the field myself, watching others, or learning about the history of it, I have always had a love for the sport. I have spent a lot of time researching, watching, and learning about the game. My two favorite events each year are Opening Day (the first day that Major League Baseball starts) and the World Series (the championships for the Major Leagues).

So, if you're hoping to learn about baseball so you can talk about it with your friends, or you want to learn the basic rules so you can learn how to play, I can help. Or maybe you just think the sport is super cool and you want to know more about it. Do you know why it's called the American pastime? How long has it been such a staple in the United States? Where did it come from? Why do people like it so much? What the heck does MLB stand for? Why do people want to go to these stadiums and watch people stand around? How come all these players you see are so dirty when they're done playing baseball? Who in the world are the Yankees? Why do people keep talking about Babe Ruth and Mickey Mantle?

If you're already a fan (or even if you're not), you will learn about the famous teams and why they are great. You'll learn about the players that make people want to hoard cards and baseballs that were hit by them. You'll even learn about the Minor Leagues, where some of those famous players made their start. We'll learn about how players get 'drafted' and what that even means.

In this book, you can learn about all things baseball. I will outline the rules and positions of baseball, explain when it was invented and where it came from, as well as tell you about some of the best players and coaches of all time. I will also share some of the coolest facts and records about baseball, and tell you how the sport has changed over the years. Next, I will explain the difference between Major and Minor Leagues and the teams in each, the popularity of baseball in places other than the United States, and some pretty amazing historical moments in baseball's most important game: The World Series. Finally, we'll break down some of the movies you may have heard of (or even watched). Why are these movies so popular? How can a movie about a baseball player bring people to tears? Why in the world do people always say "You're killin' me Smalls!"? What does it mean?

Since I began my journey of learning all things baseball, it has been my goal to share my knowledge with the world. My hope is that you will learn everything you need to know about the sport in this book so you may pass on your knowledge and love of the sport to others, and have fun in the process!

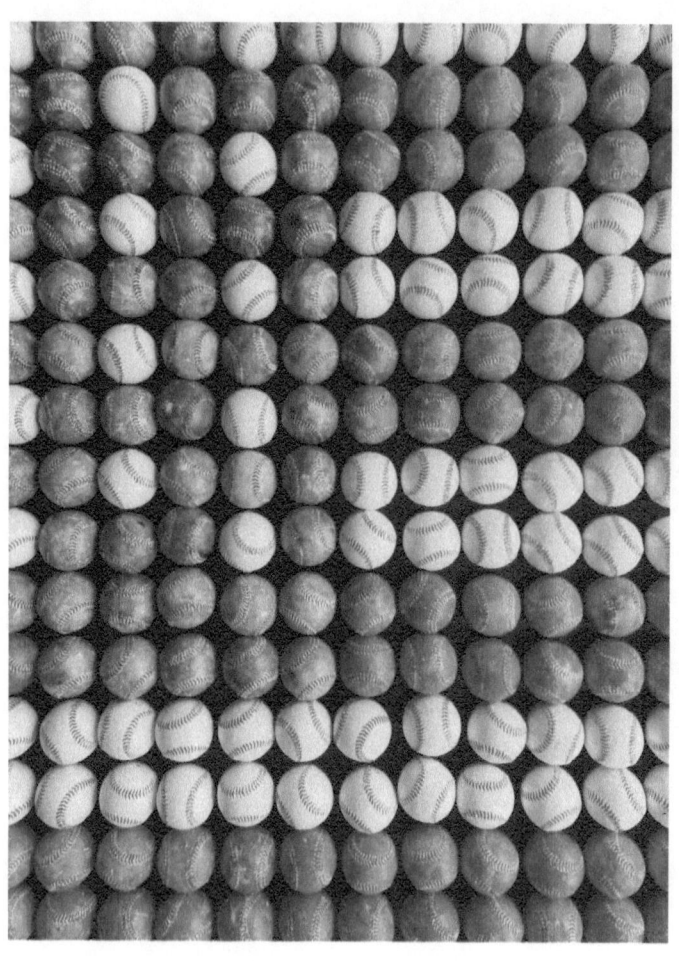

An American Flag made from baseballs.

Chapter 1
What Is Baseball?

---※---

Baseballs, left on the dirt on a baseball field.

America gets the credit for developing several sports: basketball, baseball, and gridiron football, to name a few. Baseball, though, is arguably one of the most famous of these inventions. Since the Civil War, it has been known as the 'American pastime,' even as it becomes more popular in Latin American and Asian countries all over the world.

In baseball, you play with a bat, a small, round ball, and a glove. There are nine positions on the field for defense, where all players wear gloves so they can catch the ball. Batters also wear helmets to protect their head when they face down the Pitcher, and the Catcher, the player positioned behind the batter, wears a chest plate, helmet, face mask, shin guards, and knee guards.

As for offense, the other team has a long bat, typically made of wood or aluminum. The batter tries to hit the ball out of reach of the gloved players in the field. Once the ball is hit, the player runs around the diamond-shaped field and touches the bases as they go. There are four bases, with the fourth one being Home Plate. Once a player touches the preceding three and makes it to Home, they score one point. Players can stop at any base and do not have to run through all three bases at once. If a player *does* make it all the way to Home in one hit, it is called a Home Run. Another way to get a Home Run is to hit the ball *out of the park*, meaning that the ball is hit beyond the fence of the field where the defense cannot gain control of the ball. The team with the most runs (points) at the end of nine innings (times at bat) wins the game.

For defense, the gloved players try to catch the ball hit by the batter. If the batter is tagged before they touch the base, they are considered *out* and they leave the field. If a fielder catches the baseball in the air before the ball ever hits the ground, that is also considered an out. Another way to get an out is called a *force out*. When a batter is running to a base and has no option to go back to the previous base, the fielder can touch the base while holding the ball instead of tagging the actual runner, and that counts as an out. Force outs happen when a batter is running to First Base, or when a runner has another runner on the base behind them. In other words, if a runner is standing on First Base when the ball is hit by the batter, there is a force out on both First and Second Base. The other way to get an out for the defense falls on the Pitcher. If the Pitcher throws balls that land in the preset area, called the *strike zone*, but the batter fails to hit the ball three times in a single at-bat, that is called a *strike*. The defense must get three outs, in one of the ways mentioned above, before their team can get a chance to bat.

Baseball Fielding Positions

There are nine fielding positions in baseball. Their job is to get the three outs needed to get a chance to bat for their team. The nine positions are:

1. Pitcher
2. Catcher
3. First Base
4. Second Base
5. Third Base
6. Shortstop

7. Right Field
8. Centerfield
9. Left Field

Furthermore, the baseball field is divided into the Infield and the Outfield. These positions are scattered throughout the field. Here is a picture of a baseball field so you have a better idea of what I'm talking about.

The Infield

The Infield contains the first six of the positions listed above. They are located on the dirt-covered area of the diamond-shaped field. Players playing in the Infield must throw with excellent accuracy. Their job is to tag out runners to keep the opposing team from scoring runs.

The hope of the players in the Infield is to keep the ball from getting past them into the Outfield behind them. They must expertly field the balls hit to them and keep the play in their control. This gives the runners less of a chance to make it around the bases and make it to Home Plate, and also makes getting the runners out easier.

The Pitcher

The pitcher is responsible for throwing the baseball to the batter. They are located in the very center of the Infield, on top of a small, raised hill called the *pitcher's mound*. You will also hear people refer to it as 'the mound' or the 'the hill.' Every individual play begins with the Pitcher. They stand on a Pitcher's mound in the very center of the diamond-shaped field. They must throw the ball through the *strike zone*, where the batter gets the chance to swing and hit it. The strike zone is an area between the knees and shoulders of the batter, and within the borders of the Home Plate. If the batter misses, it is a strike. Three strikes means the batter is out, and it counts as one of the three outs the defense needs to switch to offense

If the Pitcher does not throw the ball into the strike zone and the batter does not swing at it, the pitch is called a *ball*. In general, the batter shouldn't swing at the ball because it is not in the predetermined area. If the Pitcher throws four balls, the batter gets the chance to go to First Base without being tagged out by the fielders.

Once batters have made it to a base, the other job of the Pitcher is to try and keep the runner from advancing. During baseball, the runner can try to *steal* a base. A Pitcher must keep an eye on the runner and throw the ball to the appropriate fielder to try and tag the runner out. If they are successful, this counts as one of the three required outs. When this happens, it is called a *pickoff* on the part of the Pitcher.

Pitchers throw various types of pitches at different speeds. Some of these pitches include: the *fastball*, *curveball*, *slider*, *change-up*, and *knuckleball*.

The most popular of these is the fastball. Some of the best Pitchers can throw the ball at nearly 100 miles per hour (*Baseball Positions*, 2020). Of these, one of the most difficult to throw is the curveball, and it is hard to hit as well, if thrown correctly. This is because, when the Pitcher successfully uses this pitch, the ball begins to curve away from the batter at the last minute. The batter can be tricked by the movement of the ball and miss the ball. Consider all that the batter must be aware of when at bat! The ball is coming at them at 90 miles per hour and they have to judge if it's in the strike zone, should they swing, will it curve away from them at the last minute … that's a lot to evaluate in very little time!

Finally, when a ball is thrown to a Pitcher, the play is stopped. No runners may advance to the next base once the play is ceased.

Pitchers must be careful. They can suffer shoulder injuries from the extended use of their throwing arm. Shoulder injuries are painful and difficult to recover from. Serious ones usually lead to the end of the Pitcher's season, and sometimes even their career.

In order to protect their arm, Pitchers must 'warm up' before joining the game. In professional baseball, you will see Pitchers warming up with a pitching coach or teammate, possibly the Catcher. Warming up is simple: they casually throw the ball back and forth with someone else, throwing the ball faster and harder each time. They'll also stretch to keep their muscles loose. This warm-up usually takes place in something called a *bullpen*, which is a small area to the side of the field closed off from the other players. In recreational baseball, you will likely see Pitchers warming up with Catchers directly on the field before the batter takes his position.

All players should do a proper warm up before playing the game, but it's most important for the Pitcher.

The Catcher

The catcher's job is to crouch behind Home Plate and catch the ball thrown by the Pitcher. You can find them across the field from the Pitcher's mound, facing the Pitcher. When the batter misses, or the ball is thrown outside the strike zone, the Catcher must stop the motion of the ball to keep runners from trying to steal bases. Like the Pitcher, the Catcher can also throw the ball to other fielders to try and tag out those runners. The Catcher is also responsible for guarding Home Plate when the runners are trying to score. Fielders will try to throw the ball to the Catcher so they can tag the runner out and keep them from scoring a point.

The Catcher must also keep a good relationship with the Pitcher in order to tell which pitches are being thrown. It is important for the Catcher to know what pitch will be thrown in order to be able to catch it properly. Sometimes, the coach or manager will signal to the Catcher which pitch to throw, and the Catcher will in turn signal the Pitcher. Signals are used to keep the batter from knowing which pitch is being thrown. If the batter were to know, it could offer them an unfair advantage against the defense.

Other times, the Pitcher decides their own pitches and the Catcher uses signals to ask which one they choose. The pitcher will shake their head or nod to answer the Catcher, so they are both prepared for what type of pitch is being thrown. Every team has different signals for different pitches. Once, the Houston Astros were caught in a cheating scandal for trying to steal pitching signals from other teams to have an advantage.

The Catcher is often considered one of the hardest positions in baseball to play. They are the only defensive player that can see the entire field from the perspective of the batter. They also have to hold a difficult crouching position for a long period of time, while wearing heavy protective equipment. They crouch behind the batter, so the equipment they wear is incredibly important for the Catcher's safety, as the ball or the bat can hit the player and cause injuries.

A catcher in all his equipment.

First Baseman

The First Baseman is in charge of guarding the first base that batters run to after hitting the ball. They are positioned to the right of the Catcher and standing behind and to the left of the Pitcher. When a ball is hit, fielders throw the ball to the First Baseman so they can tag the runner out. The First Baseman can tag the base or the player to get the out.

First Baseman is a stressful position. They have the ball thrown to them very frequently, as every play has a batter running toward First, and they are charged with being sure to catch the ball every time. When they fail to catch the ball, it gives the runner a chance to bypass First Base and keep running to the next base. The First Baseman gets most of the action during a game, other than the Pitcher and Catcher. There is always a force out at First Base, because the batter always has to go there before they can advance. However, despite how often the ball is thrown to First, the ball isn't usually hit toward this baseman because most batters are right-handed. They must also have a strong throwing arm to be able to throw the ball across the field to the Third Baseman or the Catcher.

Second Baseman

The Second Baseman guards Second Base. They are positioned behind the Pitcher, facing their back. They usually stand between First Base and Second Base. This position requires the player to be quick on their feet, ready to field a ball at a moment's notice. Their position on the field is a common place where the ball is hit, and they have to quickly throw it to First Base to get the force out. Second Basemen also catch the most *double plays*, in which two runners are tagged out in the same individual play.

Second Basemen also need to backup the Pitcher. When the Catcher throws the ball back, there is a chance the Pitcher will miss the catch. Second Basemen should always be ready to catch the ball, in order to prevent runners from stealing bases when the ball is not in control.

Finally, Second Base is the base that runners most commonly try to steal whenever they get the chance. It is harder for a Catcher to stop runners stealing second than it is for Third Base because of how far they have to throw the ball. Also, because it is behind the Pitcher, it is hard for the Pitcher to notice when a runner tries to steal Second. They also have the most force outs, after the First Baseman.

Third Baseman

The Third Baseman guards Third Base. They are positioned to the left of the Catcher, standing behind and to the right of the Pitcher. Many batters do their best to hit the ball in the direction of Third Base, as this allows the runner more time to make it to First Base before they can be tagged out. Many balls are also hit this way because of the abundance of right-handed batters. This means the Third Baseman must have a very strong throwing arm to make the throw across the field to First Base. Third Base is the last base before Home Plate, so the Third Baseman must be careful not to let anyone past them.

Like the Second Baseman, the Third Baseman must be quick on their feet. The area near Third Base is known as the *hot corner* because many balls hit to this area come off the bat quickly and powerfully. They must be quick enough to field the ball and throw it to First Base, as well as tag their own base or the runner trying to get to it. They are also the last line of defense before Home Plate and the Catcher, so they feel a lot of pressure to stop runners in their tracks.

<u>Shortstop</u>

Shortstop plays between Second and Third Base, behind and to the left of the Pitcher. Their job is to cover Second when the Second Baseman is busy fielding the ball. They also play a 'cutoff man' for the outfielders when the ball is hit beyond the previously mentioned players. This means that when the ball is hit far out into the grass, the Shortstop will go out into the grass for the Outfielders (usually Left or Centerfield) to throw the ball to. The Shortstop in turn throws the ball to either Second or Third Base to tag out runners. They are also positioned in the aforementioned hot corner so they have a lot to do during the game.

Shortstops are also responsible for tagging out runners trying to steal Second or Third Base. They backup the Second Baseman when the ball is being thrown to them on the field.

It is also quite important for the Shortstop to be quick and athletic. They need to be able to field the ball when it comes their way, as well as have a strong arm to throw the ball from the Outfield when they are acting as the cutoff man.

The Outfield

Players standing on the Outfield

The Outfield contains three positions: Right Fielder, Center Fielder, and Left Fielder. They are located in the grass beyond the diamond shape that makes up the Infield. They catch the most *fly balls* (balls that are caught in the air before they hit the ground, which means an immediate out).

Players in the Outfield must have incredibly strong throwing arms and excellent accuracy. When the ball is hit all the way to them, catching the ball is the most important thing they need to do. The second most important thing is for them to throw the ball back to the infield in case other runners need to be tagged out. In many cases, they are the last line of defense to prevent a Home Run.

Right Fielder

Right Fielders are positioned in the Outfield behind the First Baseman. Other than catching the ball and throwing it back to the Infield, Right Fielders should backup the First Baseman. When the ball is thrown to the First Baseman, the Right Fielder should be close behind them in order to catch any missed balls and regain control of the play. This leads to fewer bases stolen and fewer runs scored.

Like the First Basemen, Right Fielders need to have some of the strongest throwing arms. They have to cover a lot of ground in the Outfield and need to be able to throw the ball to Third. However, since most batters are right-handed, Right Field is where the least amount of balls are hit. However, when a left-handed player is up to bat, the Right Fielder should be ready for anything, as any ball hit long will be headed directly for right field.

Center Fielder

Center Fielders are positioned in the middle of the Outfield, in the grass directly behind Second Base. Center Fielders are the leaders of the players in the Outfield. Every time a fly ball is hit into the Outfield and the players are not sure which player should catch it, the Center Fielder is responsible for catching the ball, or for calling the ball for the Right or Left Fielder to catch. Calling the ball is very important because when the players are looking up to the sky at the ball, they risk running into each other and causing injuries.

The Center Fielder is also one of the fastest players on the team. They have a lot of ground to cover in the Outfield and they need to be quick enough to cover it. Many Home Runs are scored by hitting the ball into centerfield, so the player in that position must be prepared to field the ball quickly and get the ball back to the infield (usually the Shortstop, if the ball has gone far into the grass). If the ball is hit over their head, they need to be fast enough to chase down the ball, and strong enough to throw the ball back to the Infield.

Left Fielder

The Left Fielder is positioned in the grass behind Third Base, typically settled between the Third Baseman and the Shortstop, in that same hot corner as the two formerly mentioned infielders. Many balls are hit to Left Field because so many batters are right-handed.

Left Fielders are one of the few players who do not need a very strong throwing arm. They rarely need to make the throw to First Base, usually only needing to throw the ball to Third Base or to the Shortstop. In the event that the ball is hit over the Left Fielder's head, the Shortstop follows them into the grass to shorten the distance the Left Fielder must throw the ball.

The Batter

Although the batter is not technically a position like the ones we just listed, it's still important to talk about. Batters have an important job: to score. Hitting a tiny ball flying at you at 100 miles an hour is no small feat, either, nor is hitting it far and fast enough to keep the fielders from catching it.

Batters take their position between the Pitcher and the Catcher. If they are right-handed, they stand to the right of Home Plate, the left of the Catcher. Their dominant hand is toward the Catcher, as the power of their swing will come from pushing the bat across Home Plate to hit the ball. Left-handers stand on the other side of the plate, with their right side facing the Pitcher.

When the ball is thrown through the strike zone, a batter takes their swing. The bat is long, thin towards the grip (where the batter holds the bat), and thick and round towards the end. The batter wants the ball to hit the thick end of the bat, otherwise they risk injury to their hand. It also allows for more power and a better hit.

When the batter hits the ball, they drop the bat and take off running: not throw the bat, but drop it. If a batter throws the bat over their shoulder before running, they can be considered out by the umpire because of the possible danger it can cause. Most batters simply let the bat fall from their hand after swinging, so it drops safely to the ground behind them.

They have to run towards First, waiting for their coach—or in some cases a teammate—to tell them to either stop at First or continue to Second. Another coach or player stands near Third, and they will tell the runner to either stop at Second or keep going to Third (they are also responsible for telling the runner to stop at Third or keep going to Home Plate). These coaches must watch the ball and tell their player if the ball is in control of the fielders or not, so the runner can focus on running and not trying to find the ball in the field.

When a batter is waiting their turn, they usually stand in a predetermined area on the field, in foul territory. You'll hear people refer to that batter as being *on deck*. When a batter is done with their turn, they either go to a base (if the hit is good) or return to the *dugout* (if they struck out), which is the place where players sit during the time they are not on the field. If they hit the ball and go to a base, they leave the bat at Home Plate. Usually, the next batter will grab the bat and toss it (carefully) back to the dugout to be put away. In the Major Leagues, an employee for the team will usually grab the bat instead of the next batter.

Bases

A picture of a base on a field.

Before we get into the rules of baseball, I want to talk about the bases. Remember, I said that runners do not have to touch all the bases in a single hit. This means that there can be multiple runners on base at the same time. There can be a runner on First and Second, First and Third, and so forth. In the case of all three bases hosting a runner, this is referred to as *bases loaded*. This means several things for the defense.

First, every base has a force out, including Home Plate. The catcher must be ready to tag out a runner to prevent a point from being scored. Also, having a runner on Third Base runs the risk of the runner trying to steal Home Plate (though this is uncommon in Major League Baseball, MLB).

Second, the Pitcher is under a lot of pressure to keep the batter from getting a hit and bringing his teammates Home. The Pitcher must also be sure not to throw the four balls required to walk the batter to First, which would both allow the offense to score and keep the bases loaded.

Third, none of the bases can be stolen. In rare cases, you may see a runner try to steal Home from Third, but this is rare in the Major Leagues.

Finally, when the bases are loaded and the batter hits a Home Run, it means four points for the offense. This is referred to as a *Grand Slam*, and it doesn't happen often in the Major Leagues. You may also hear of something called a *ground roll double*. This occurs when a batter hits the ball out of the park, but the ball touches the ground before that happens (usually, it rolls underneath the fence). Instead of counting as a Home

Run, the batter is granted a double and advances to Second Base.

Also, for batters, there is a lot of lingo about the bases. If you hear someone refer to a batter as hitting a *single*, this means that they managed to make it to First off their hit, but they had to stop there. A *double* means they made it to Second, and a *triple* means they got to Third.

Lastly, you will see a lot of players getting dirty during the game. When running to a base or stealing one, runners often try to *slide* in order to avoid being tagged by the fielders. Sliding means that the runner falls to the ground and dives for the base, either head first or feet first. Sliding is most common at Home Plate, but can happen at any base.

A runner sliding into a base as another player tags him.

Now that you know the ins and outs of each position, the importance of the bases, and all the lingo, let's discuss the rules of baseball and how to play properly.

Rules of Baseball

The rules of baseball are various. Remembering them takes practice. There are umpires who are on the field at all times to make sure those rules are followed. Umpires decide whether the Pitcher has thrown a strike or not, they decide whether or not a runner was tagged out or made it safely to the base, and they decide whether a ball is hit into fair or foul territory. Umpires are also responsible for making sure the ball is sufficient for the game. In the Major Leagues, the life span of the ball is only about five to seven pitches. The umpire is in charge of retiring the ball (if it hasn't been given to a fan or hit out of the park) and giving the Pitcher a new one.

Fair territory is the area between the lines surrounding the edges of the baseball field. Any baseball within these lines is a *fair ball* and is therefore in play. Balls hit outside these lines are considered *foul balls* and they count as strikes against the batter, though they cannot count as the third strike. In the Major Leagues, many fans catch and keep foul balls as souvenirs. These balls can later be sold for a decent price, depending on the batter. For example, a ball hit by Babe Ruth can earn a collector a pretty sum of money.

There must be at least nine players for a team to play (most professional teams have many more). If a team lacks nine players, they must forfeit the game. All of the positions on the field *must* be filled in order to play the game.

The game is played for at least nine innings, each of which gives both teams one chance to be at bat and score runs. Sometimes, when a team is tied at the end of nine innings, extra innings are played to break the tie. The Home team (the team who normally plays at the field the game is taking place on) always takes the field first. The other team, called the *visitor*, gets to bat first. You will hear innings referred to by the *top* and *bottom*, which refers to the first or second half of the inning.

In other words, when you hear someone say "it's the top of the fifth," that means that the visiting team is at bat during the beginning of the fifth inning. On the other hand, when someone says it's the "bottom of eighth," that means the home team is at bat during the end of the eighth inning.

So, how on earth can we remember all these rules? The easiest thing to do is break them down.

Batting Rules

Those at bat must bat in a specified order set at the beginning of the game. Once a batting order is in place, it cannot be changed. However, coaches can make substitutions in the batting order, but the substitute must bat in the same place as the player they replaced. The player who takes the original batter's place is known as a *pinch hitter*. This is often done to put in a more skillful hitter for a player that has a different skill. For example, Pitchers are often not very good at batting, so they may have a pinch hitter hit for them.

A batter gets three strikes before they are out. If an umpire calls the pitch a strike, it is counted against the batter even if they do not swing at it. If they swing and miss, it is a strike whether it is in the strike zone or not. If they hit the ball into foul territory, they do not get to advance to First Base. Finally, if the ball bounces off the bat and goes behind the batter, this is called a *foul tip* and can count as the first and second strike, just like the regular kind of foul ball.

If a batter is hit with the ball thrown by the Pitcher, the batter is granted a base, assuming they are not injured. This means that they can walk to First Base without the threat of being tagged out. In the case that the batter cannot remain on the field due to injury or pain, another player can take their place on the base to run on the field. The manager is in charge of choosing a runner to take the base in place of the batter.

A batter waiting on deck for his turn.

Fielding Rules

Pitchers try to throw strikes that are too fast or too complicated for batters to hit. Their hope is to strike out all the batters without having to field any balls. When they are successful, this is called a *shut out* or a *no-hitter*.

When a ball is hit into the field, players attempt to catch the ball in the air. When this happens, the ball is considered a *fly ball*. If they catch it before it touches the ground in fair territory, this counts as one out. Three outs are needed for the teams to switch from offense to defense.

If the ball does hit the ground, it is called a *ground ball*. These require the fielders to crouch and capture the ball in their gloves. They then must tag out the runners, tag their base, or throw the ball to the correct player so they can complete that task. Stopping the ball on the ground does not count as an out, so the runner must be tagged in order to earn one of the three outs.

A fielder getting ready to catch a ground ball.

Balls hit into foul territory are discarded and the Pitcher is given a new ball to throw to the batter. No runs can be scored from a foul ball.

<u>Uniform Rules</u>

An example of what baseball caps look like.

According to the National Federation of State Highschool Associations, all uniforms on a single team should be the same color and style. They consist of shirts or a jersey, pants, a cap, and shoes. However, when a player wears protective headgear (such as a helmet) this will replace a hat. Helmets are required when players are at bat. Catchers are also required to wear helmets while they are on the field (*Baseball Uniform Rules*, 2016)

All sleeve lengths for individual players are meant to be of the same approximate length. The shirts should not be frayed or ripped. If a player wears long sleeves under their shirts, the sleeves must be black or another solid dark color. Pitchers are not allowed to wear any item on their arm or hand that may be distracting to the batter. No uniforms should have any dangerous buttons or any reflective ornaments. All players should have an individual number printed on the back of their shirt.

Only one logo is allowed on a uniform, whole or partial. It must be a small size so as not to distract other players. If there are special patches or memorial signs, they must be uniformly placed and must remain small (*Baseball Uniform Rules*, 2016).

In the MLB, though, the rules for uniforms are a bit more relaxed. You may see them wearing a necklace or even a bracelet during a game. However, they still cannot wear any polished metal or glass buttons on their uniforms.

If you've ever seen a professional baseball player, you probably saw him wearing a jersey with the colors of his team over a pair of light gray pants. However, when playing at their home field, players often wear white jerseys. Players also wear cleats, which are shoes with 10 to 12 spikes on the bottom of the sole. Cleats allow for the players to have added traction and grip on the ground while they are playing.

If you've seen a Pitcher, you may have seen him wearing a towel or rag in his front pants pocket. This allows the Pitcher to wipe his throwing hand, keeping sweaty palms from causing him to throw a bad pitch. He may have even been wearing a face mask, though this is rare for Major League Pitchers. The face masks are a good idea though. Their position is particularly close to the batter, and any ball he gets hit with could cause serious injury, especially if he is struck in the face or head.

Batters are required to wear a helmet when at bat, with at least one side covering their ear. They usually wear that ear protection on the side facing the Pitcher. For example, a left-handed batter has his right side facing the Pitcher. The ear protection on the helmet will therefore be on the right side of the helmet. For right-handed batters, it is the opposite.

As for the gloves the fielders wear, they are made of supple, sturdy, flexible leather. The leather is very thick around the palm, to protect the hand from the impact of the ball. Many players (or employees that are in charge of caring for equipment) use special oils or conditioners to keep the leather from deteriorating. Despite what many think, gloves are worn on the non-dominant hand, meaning, right-handed players wear their gloves on their left hand. This is so they can throw with their stronger arm.

Summary

So, baseball has a whole bunch of rules and positions to remember. Put simply, a pitcher throws a ball to the batter, the batter tries to hit the ball. If the batter fails, they are considered *out*. If the batter is successful, they get the chance to run the bases. Usually, batters only take one to two bases at a time. Once on a base, batters become runners. Runners are allowed to steal a base at any time, but their best chance is when the ball is not in control of the opposing team (usually when the Catcher misses the pitch). The goal of the runner is to touch all three bases before running to Home Plate to score a run.

There are nine fielding positions, all of which are charged with catching the ball hit by the batter and retiring runners (putting them out) to keep the runners from scoring. They must get three outs in order to get a chance to be at bat and score runs for their own team. Each fielding position has special requirements and they all take extensive practice to perfect.

The batters try to hit the ball on the thick part of their bat and run to as many bases as they can get to without being tagged out. They may even slide on the ground to a base to avoid being tagged.

The umpires are in charge of deciding when runners are out or *safe* (when they make it to a base before they can be tagged). They also decide whether or not a Pitcher has thrown a strike to the batter or not or if a ball was hit into fair or foul territory. There are typically two to three umpires at a baseball game.

Uniforms must be of the same style and color, with similar sleeve lengths for all players. Caps must be worn unless protective headgear is worn in their place. All players must have an individual number on their back.

Now, let's explore where baseball came from!

Chapter 2

When Was Baseball Invented?

There are references to games resembling baseball that date all the way back to the 18th century. The two games that appear to have inspired baseball are two English games: Rounders and Cricket (if you've ever watched a game of Cricket and baseball, you may notice some similarities). By the time of the American Revolution, these games were being played in various styles all around the country (*Who Invented Baseball?*, 2013).

Baseball as We Know It

In September of 1845, the New York Knickerbocker Baseball Club was founded in New York City. One of the founders, bank clerk and firefighter Alexander Joy Cartwright, created a new set of rules that would shape into the baseball game we know today. These rules made the game more fast-paced and more challenging, which made the game more entertaining overall for both players and fans.

In 1846, the Knickerbockers played the first ever baseball game against a Cricket team (*Who Invented Baseball*, 2013). Baseball has been played ever since.

Abner Doubleday

There is a well-known myth that Abner Doubleday, a Civil War hero from Cooperstown, New York, invented baseball in 1839. This story is utterly false, as Doubleday never even claimed any knowledge of baseball at the time. So, how did a myth become such a popular story among fans?

In 1907, 16 years following Doubleday's passing, a special commission, led by Major League player A. J. Spalding and president of the National League Abraham Mille, was trying to determine the origins of baseball. Specifically, the commission wanted to determine whether the game was a true American invention or if it had been derived from the English games. There was a need for the game to be considered wholly American, especially when immigrants, mainly Irish, began playing on more and more teams.

One man, Abner Graves, told the commission that he went to school with Doubleday and spread the story that Doubleday was the creator of baseball. He claimed he saw Doubleday create a diagram of a baseball field, as well as heard him name the game. Desperate to prove that baseball was not inspired by games played in other countries, Spalding and Mills spread this story across the country, and the lie stuck.

Of course, if they had tried, it would have been easy to discredit Graves's story. First, he was only 5 years old in 1839, when he claims to have been in school with Doubleday. Second, Doubleday was in Military school at West Point in 1839, and there is no record of him traveling 140 miles to Cooperstown to invent baseball. Also, Doubleday was a well-known war hero. His records are well kept and documented, yet none of those records mention baseball at any time. Finally, Mills, the President of the National League and the leader of the investigation that led to this myth, was close friends with Doubleday and never once mentioned a connection between his friend and baseball until Graves made his claims.

The Doubleday myth was so widely accepted that, when the Baseball Hall Of Fame was created in Cooperstown in the 1930s, his picture was mounted on a sign outside the building. It wasn't until recently that the discovery of the lie was made and more research into the truth was done (*Who Invented Baseball?*, 2013).

The Oldest Teams of Baseball

So, now that we know how old baseball is, how old are the teams we know and hear about today? The top 10 oldest baseball teams in the Major Leagues are as follows (*10 oldest baseball teams in America*, 2017):

1. Atlanta Braves
2. Chicago Cubs
3. St. Louis Cardinals
4. Pittsburgh Pirates
5. Cincinnati Reds
6. San Francisco Giants
7. Philadelphia Phillies
8. Los Angeles Dodgers
9. Oakland Athletics
10. Minnesota Twins

There is some conflict about the Braves being the oldest team in the Major Leagues, as the first recorded professional baseball team was the Cincinnati Red Stockings. This was the first team to pay their players and call themselves a wholly professional team.

The Red Stockings, now known as the Cincinnati Reds, were formed in 1866. They became an openly professional team in 1869, with 10 players being paid a salary (it's thought that some teams were secretly paying their players before then). However, they did not become the Reds (the team we know today) until 1881, and did not enter the MLB until 1882.

The Braves

The Atlanta Braves, however, formed in 1871 and joined the MLB in 1876. As the team joined the MLB before the Reds, it is officially considered the oldest team in Major League Baseball. The Braves weren't always in Atlanta though, nor were they always the

Braves. They started in Boston as the Red Stockings before their name changed to Red Caps, then Beaneaters, Doves, Braves, and Bees. They moved to Milwaukee and became the Braves again before they went to Atlanta. They play there today and they have kept the name ever since.

The Cubs

The Chicago Cubs follow closely behind the Braves, as this team was also formed in 1871 and joined the MLB in 1876. Unlike the Braves, the Cubs have always been in Chicago. However, their name was originally the White Stockings (there is another MLB team today known as the Chicago White Sox), before their name was changed to the Colts and then the Orphans before they became the Cubs.

The Cardinals

The next team to join the MLB was the St. Louis Cardinals. The team was formed in 1882 and joined the Major Leagues the same year. They have always been in St. Louis, under the names of the Brown Stockings, the Browns, and the Perfectos.

The Pirates

The fourth oldest team is the Pittsburgh Pirates. They became a team in 1881, so they are technically older than the Cardinals, but they did not join the MLB until 1882 after the cardinals had already joined. They only have one other previous name: Allegheny.

The Reds

Following the Pirates is the Cincinnati Reds. Though they were the first professional team, they did not become the team they are today until 1881. They joined the MLB in 1882 alongside the Pirates and the Cardinals. They were formerly known as the Red Stockings and the Redlegs.

The Giants

The sixth oldest team in the Major leagues are the San Francisco Giants. They were established as a team in 1883 and joined the MLB the same year. They were formerly the New York Gothams, then the New York Giants before moving to San Francisco, where they kept their name.

The Phillies

Sitting at number seven is the Philadelphia Phillies. This team was also formed in 1883, and joined the MLB alongside the Giants. They have always been in Philadelphia and have only been known by one previous name: the Quakers.

The Dodgers

Following the Phillies are the Los Angeles Dodgers. They were formed in 1883 and joined in 1884. They were formerly of Brooklyn under the names of Atlantic's, Grays, Bridegrooms, Grooms, Superbas, Trolley Dodgers, and the Dodgers before they became the Los Angeles Dodgers.

The Athletics

In 1901, the Oakland Athletics became the ninth oldest team. They entered the MLB in 1901, formerly known as the Philadelphia Athletics and the Kansas City Athletics.

The Twins

Finally, the same year, the Minnesota Twins joined the MLB. They were formerly known as the Washington Senators and the Washington Nationals (there is another team called the Washington Nationals today, but they are younger than the Twins) (*10 oldest baseball teams in America*, 2017).

The Major League

You're probably wondering what all these terms mean: 'National League,' 'MLB,' and 'Major League,' to name a few. Well, there's a lot of history surrounding these organizations as well.

To recap, the first official baseball game was played in Hoboken, New Jersey, in 1846. Then, the Cincinnati Red Stockings became the first openly professional baseball team. In 1871, the National Association of Professional Baseball Players was formed. This Association was the first established 'Major League' (top-tier professional) baseball team.

The National League

Five years later in 1876, William Hulbert created the National League of Professional Baseball Clubs in Chicago. He wanted his League to replace the Association, because he believed the organization was corrupt. This League later became known as the *National League*, and it is still called that today (*This day in history*, 2009).

The eight original members of the National League were the Boston Red Stockings (Atlanta Braves), Chicago White Stockings (Chicago Cubs), Cincinnati Red Stockings, (Cincinnati Reds), Hartford Dark Blues, Philadelphia Athletics (Oakland Athletics), and the St. Louis Brown Stockings (St. Louis Cardinals).

The American League

In 1901, the American League of Professional Baseball Clubs was founded. They became a rival of the National League, and in 1903, the best team from each league began playing in the World Series.

Black Leagues

Before 1947, Black players were not permitted to play in the MLB due to segregation laws during that time. However, there are many Black players who had extreme talent and wanted to play the beloved game. The Black League was founded in 1920 and became known as the *Negro Major League*.

Even after the Civil War ended, racism was still a major problem in the United States. Black players were not allowed to play baseball with the White players. So, the Black players formed their own teams. The first ever documented game between two Black teams was played in November of 1859 in New York City. The teams were the Henson Baseball Club of Jamaica, Queens, and the Unknowns Weekesville of Brooklyn. The Henson Club were the victors.

At the end of the 1860s, the biggest area for Black baseball teams was in Philadelphia. James H. Francis and Francis Wood, two former cricket players, founded the Pythian Baseball Club. This club played often in Camden, New Jersey, near the ferry landing because it was hard to get permits to play baseball in the city itself. The promoter of this club, named Octavius Catto, applied to be a part of the National Association of Baseball Players, but was denied due to his race. The association went on to exclude any baseball club with a Black player.

In the 1870s, professional Black baseball players began to arise. The first known professional Black player was Bud Fowler, who played for the Chelsea, Massachusetts team and then the Lynn, Massachusetts team in the International Association, a Minor League. The American Association, considered a professional Major League at the time, featured Moses Fleetwood Walker and Welday Wilberforce Walker, two brothers who became the first Black Major League players.

The first ever professional Black baseball team was the Cuban Giants, formed in 1885. The team was formed when Keystone Athletics of Philadelphia and the Orion's of Philadelphia merged with the Manhattans of Washington, DC. The first ever league for these teams was the *National Colored Baseball League*, but it was set up as a Minor League. However, the League did not last long due to low attendance. The teams included in this League were the Baltimore Lord Baltimores, Boston Resolutes, Louisville Fall City, New York Gorhams, Philadelphia Pythians, and the Pittsburgh Keystones. Two more teams joined later, but never played a game with the League. They were the Cincinnati Browns and the Washington Capital Cities.

The Cuban Giants were quite popular, which led to some other teams emerging with similar names. Teams with the names of the Cuban X-Giants, the Genuine Cuban Giants, the Columbia Giants, and the Brooklyn Royal Giants were a few of these teams. Despite having 'Cuban' in their name, the players for the teams were Black Americans. They chose the name in hopes to lessen criticism, as the United States and Cuba were on good terms then. Later, in 1899, actual Cuban teams would come to play in North America, consisting of White and Black players. Ironically, during the time of segregation, dark-skinned Cubans and Dominicans were allowed to play on White teams, when American Black players were not.

In 1888, a man named Frank Leland got a permit to play at South Side Park for his team in the Union Baseball Club, with the help of some Black businessmen who sponsored the team. The park was a 5,000-seat facility and was quite successful, eventually going professional and becoming the Chicago Unions.

In 1920, the Negro National League was founded. The League was composed of eight teams: The Chicago American Giants, Chicago Giants, Cuban Stars, Dayton Marcos, Detroit Stars, Indianapolis ABCs, Kansas City Monarchs, and the St. Louis Giants. On May 2nd, the Indianapolis ABCs beat the Chicago Giants.

In 1941, when the United States entered World War II, Black baseball players were not spared joining the war effort. However, because many players over 30 were considered too old to serve, the Black Leagues did not suffer as much as the White Major League teams did. The stadiums for these games became packed as the Black League games became largely popular with fans across the country. In 1942, the Negro World Series came around and the Black teams thrived.

In 1945, a committee to desegregate baseball was formed. However, a member of this committee who was against integration stalled this process, and the committee never formally met. Another member, Branch Rickey, told people he planned to create an all Black League and sent scouts across the United States, Mexico, and Puerto Rico to find the perfect player to bring into the MLB. This is how he found Jackie Robinson.

Robinson was 'tested' by Rickey when Rickey berated him and called him racial slurs, telling him that this is what he would face in the Major League should he decide to play. Robinson passed this test. Then, the Fair Employment Practices Act was passed that prohibited discrimination in hiring. This led to the public announcement that Jackie Robinson would be signed to play in the White Major Leagues. Robinson made his debut in 1947.

As more and more Black players were signed to play Major League Baseball and the sport was largely integrated, the Black Leagues began to lose fans. The interest in those teams fizzled until the Black Leagues ceased to exist in 1966.

Women's Leagues

There has never been a woman to play Major League Baseball. However, in 1943, the All-American Girls Professional Baseball League (AAGPBL) was founded. The League hosted over 600 women players, spread across 10 teams in the American Midwest. The League was founded by Phillip K. Wrigley and lasted from 1943 to 1954.

The League was founded to keep public interest in baseball during World War II, when most of the men who played for the MLB were off fighting in the war. Like the men's League, this League was also segregated.

Two-hundred women were scouted from amateur softball teams and invited to try out at Wrigley Field, where the Chicago Cubs played; 60 of those women were chosen for the roster. The players were selected by skill, but also needed to be the 'ideal feminine' player to please fans. The first game in this League was played on May 30th, 1943. In 1944, the six team National Girls Baseball League was founded with Chicano area teams. The two Leagues rivaled each other for players over the years until they made an agreement not to steal players from each other in 1946.

The AAGPBL's first season started with the players using a softball instead of a baseball. The Pitcher's mound was moved from regulation baseball's 60 feet, 6 inches to 40 feet from the Home Plate. The distance between the bases was 65 feet, which was longer than in softball but 25 feet shorter than in men's baseball. The Pitchers threw the ball underhanded in a windmill motion rather than over their heads. However, both men's and women's teams played with nine players on the field and threw from a Pitcher's mound (softball players throw from a flat surface). By 1948, the ball had shrunk a bit, the Pitcher's mound was moved back, and the distance between bases was lengthened. Even after that, the rules continued to approach those of baseball until the Pitcher's mound was back at 60 feet, the distance between bases was at 85 feet (only 5 feet shorter than men's baseball), and the women threw a regulation baseball.

Women had to wear a belted, tunic style dress as a uniform. The regulation stated that the flared skirt could not be more than 6 inches above the knee, but this rule was usually ignored because shorter skirts made it easier to run.

During spring training, the women had to attend classes that taught them about proper hygiene, manners, and dress code. They each received a beauty kit and were taught how to use it, because the women were expected to be as attractive as possible. They were not allowed to have short hair, could not smoke or drink in public places, could not wear pants, and had to wear lipstick at all times. Players who did not follow these rules were fined, and the amount increased with each offense. In 1944, one player named Josephine D'Angelo was fired for cutting her hair short. Each team was assigned a male chaperone by the League, and the players' contracts were much stricter about personal conduct than those of the male players.

The women's League became very popular over the years, peaking in 1948 when 10 teams brought in 910,000 paying spectators. The Rockford Peaches won the most championships with four wins, followed by the Milwaukee/Grand Rapids Chicks with three. The South Bend Blue Sox and the Racine Belles both won two championships, and Kalamazoo Lassies won one in their final season in 1954.

A movie made in 1992, called *A League of Their Own* and starring Madonna, Geena Davis, and Tom Hanks, tells the story of this League and the teams who played on it at this time. It is a must see and discussed further in Chapter 11.

Newer Teams

There were many teams who came in and out of the National League, but it remained an eight-team league until 1962, when the New York Mets and the Houston Colt .45s (now the Houston Astros) joined. The San Diego Padres and the Montreal Expos (now the current Washington Nationals) joined the League in 1969. That same year, the League was divided into East and West Divisions, each of which had six teams.

Later, in 1993, the Colorado Rockies and the Florida Marlins joined the League, followed by the Arizona Diamondbacks in 1998. In 1994, the League added a Central Division.

In 1997, the Major League allowed play between the National League and American League, so long as the teams were in the same division (East, West, or Central). They changed the rules in 2002 to allow teams in different divisions to play each other as well. The inter-league game between the Chicago White Sox and the Chicago Cubs is one of the most watched games by fans in the MLB.

The biggest difference between the two leagues is that the American League has a rule, established in 1973, that allows for teams to switch a Pitcher for a designated hitter in the batting lineup to allow for better scoring (most Pitchers don't hit well). This results in teams in the American League usually scoring more runs than those in the National League, which some fans believe makes a more entertaining game.

Evolution of Baseball

Baseball has been around for 130 years. Since its invention, the game has been through many changes, such as different positions, uniform and team changes, and had several rules added. So, what's the difference between baseball *then* and baseball *now*? The next section will talk about the way the game has changed, how it happened, and why.

The Actual Baseball

Old baseballs before the MLB changed the requirements.

The baseball we play with today is not the same as it used to be. Today, the baseball is made with wool yarn and wrapped in cowhide, weighs 5 ounces, and has a circumference of 9 centimeters. They were originally made with horsehide, up until 1976 (*Evolution of sport—Baseball*, 2015).

The other change, made in the early 1900s, was weighing and measuring balls. Before then, balls were not tightly wound in the cowhide and did not have to be weighed before use. Some batters could even hit the ball so hard that the hide would be torn off the ball. Pitchers could alter the weight of balls with spit or tar to have an advantage on the batter. In 1920, the rules were changed because a batter named Roy Chapman died after being struck in the head with a ball altered by the Pitcher. Chapman is the only player to have died after being struck by a pitch. Weighing the balls has kept players honest and made sure batters and fielders remain safe.

The number of balls used in a game has also changed. From 1900 to 1919, Major League games only used about five or six balls a game. This was known as the 'dead ball era' because balls that have been hit several times and have been covered in grass and dirt are harder to hit. It was also referred to this way because the balls were more difficult to hit, making Home Runs and hits in general fewer than what they are now. This gave Pitchers an advantage over the batters. Now, a Major League game uses 50 to 60 balls a game, partially because fans keep balls that are hit into the stands as souvenirs. Also, umpires pull a ball out of play once it has struck the dirt a few times. Sometimes in Major League games, you may even see a kind player toss a ball he caught up to a nearby fan.

The Baseball Bat

Baseball and glove.

When the National League was first founded, baseball players could play with any bat they chose. Over time, the width of the bat became regulated, until it reached the final point of 2.61 inches.

In 1869, the maximum length for a bat became 42 inches, which is still the rule today. However, the typical standard for players today is 33 to 34 inches long. The shorter bat is easier to swing and easier to maneuver than the long ones they used to play with.

In the beginnings of baseball, players could use a bat with a flat side to hit the ball, but the rules required the bat to be round as of 1893.

In the Major League, players are required to use wooden bats (recreational teams typically use aluminum bats). The wood can be either ash, maple, or birch. There is no weight requirement on bats, but they cannot be 3.5 ounces lighter than the length of the bat (*Evolution of sport—Baseball*, 2015).

The Outfield

Some owners of professional teams and managers have made some changes of their own for their specific teams. One of these would include the length of the Outfield on their home field. Most team owners have made a decision to shorten the Outfield over time in order to allow for more home runs to be hit in a game, which excites fans and encourages attendance to their games.

For example, when Fenway Park was opened in 1912, the distance to the fence around the Outfield was 488 feet. Today, that distance is only 420 feet (*Evolution of sport—Baseball*, 2015).

Designated Hitter

As mentioned before, there was no such position as Designated Hitter before 1973, when the American League created the position. Like shortening the Outfield, having a Designated Hitter allowed for more

Home Runs to be hit and led to more excitement from fans.

This position also increases the career time of the individual batter, because they do not have to use their skills elsewhere on the field.

The first year that this position was used, hits in the American League went up by 2,500, allowing for quite the exciting game (*Evolution of sport—Baseball*, 2015).

The Use of Technology

Like it does with most everything, technology has caused several changes in the game of baseball. In 2002, video technology was used at the Home Plate to track pitch speed and location.

Between 2002 and 2014, video replay was rarely used to dispute calls made by the umpire unless it happened at Home Plate. However, in 2014, the rules were expanded to cover the rest of the field. Now, managers can use video replay to challenge a call once in a game. Usually, the challenge is made on whether or not a runner made it to the base before being tagged out or not.

The other benefit of using video technology and replay is umpire accuracy. Umpires can review their calls if they are unsure and make decisions properly, so their calls are more accurate. Before the video, the umpire accuracy average was 83%. Now, that number is closer to 87% (*Evolution of sport—Baseball*, 2015).

Summary

Wow! Baseball has a whole lot of history. If you wanted to, you can even go farther back in time to discover the origins of Cricket and Rounders, the games that inspired baseball. For example, the flat bat used by baseball players in the early days were likely inspired by the flat bat used by Cricket players.

We have Alexander Cartwright to thank for the original code of rules for baseball as we know it today, and not Abner Doubleday, who never had anything to do with baseball and never even claimed to.

The Atlanta Braves are the oldest team in MLB, though the Cincinnati Red Stockings are credited with being the first openly professional team that paid their players a salary.

The National League was founded in 1876, by William Hulbert. The American League formed and became their rival in 1901, and the two leagues began competing in the World Series starting in 1903. The two leagues did not play each other outside of the Series until 1997, and then different divisions played each other starting in 2002. The biggest difference between the two leagues is that the American League has the Designated Hitter position, established in 1973.

Baseball has evolved a lot since its invention in 1845. Balls are made with cowhide instead of horsehide, they are weighed, and pitchers cannot alter the weight of the ball for their advantage anymore. More balls are used during a single game now than used to be used. This makes for both a safer and more exciting game.

Bats are regulated too, by weight, length, and composition. Players get to choose the wood their bats are made of, and typically choose shorter ones to have a better chance at hitting the ball.

Most managers in the Major League have decided to have their Outfield shortened in order for their teams to hit more home runs and impress fans. Designated Hitters are also in place now to allow for a more exciting game. One cool fact is that the Boston Red Sox host a tall wall in their Outfield, known as the 'Big Green Monster.' It's called this because it is difficult to hit the ball over that wall, but many batters strive to do so when they play on that field.

Finally, technology has significantly changed the game in terms of fairness for the players and accuracy for the umpires. Managers can make challenges on calls that they disagree with. However, the umpire still has the final say on the call. Too much arguing with the umpire can lead to players or managers being thrown out of the game.

So, now that we know where baseball comes from and what it's like today, what's next? The next thing to learn about are the greatest players of all time! Let's see who made this game so cool.

Chapter 3
The Best Players in Every Position

A batter, moments before he hits the ball.

Remember those positions we learned about in Chapter 1? Those positions all come with their own challenges and difficulties. Have you ever wondered who played those? Well, there are several players who played in those positions and made their career by being the best. Let's take a look at the best players in their home positions.

Best Players

For the next section, we will break down some of the most famous players in each position, based on both their offensive (batting) abilities and defensive (fielding) abilities. Obviously not all who should be listed here can be, but these are a few of the big names worth noting as a start. You can always look up other names on your own!

Catcher

Josh Gibson

Gibson was known as the 'Black Babe Ruth' and is a member of the Baseball Hall Of Fame. His plaque mentions that he hit "almost 800" Home Runs in his 17-year-long career. Unfortunately, Gibson played in the segregated league we discussed in Chapter 2 at the time, and his league did not keep comprehensive records. This means that no one knows his actual stats for his entire career.

Johnny Bench

Johnny Bench played in the Major League for 17 seasons, hit 389 Home Runs, and won two most valuable player (MVP) awards in his career. He was named Rookie of the Year in 1968. As for playing Catcher, he was well known for his strong throwing arm and ability to work with his Pitchers. He was given 10 awards for his defensive abilities.

Yogi Berra

Here's a name you may have heard. This guy holds the record for winning more World Series as a player than anyone else in MLB history. He played for 19 seasons, 18 of which were with the New York Yankees. He was also an 18-time All-Star player and is one of six players to win the MVP award three times. Later in his life, he went on to become a manager for the Yankees and the Mets. He won three World Series as a manager. He was inducted into the Hall of Fame in 1972. Along with his great record, Berra is best known for his colorful and amusing use of nonsense phrases, such as: "It ain't over till it's over," "Baseball is 90% mental and the other half is physical," and "I never said most of the things I said."

Pitcher

Cy Young

Cy Young is known as the best right-handed Pitcher. He is the namesake for the Cy Young award, which is given to the best Pitcher in each league at the end of the year. Young's career ended with 511 wins, he was the starting Pitcher for 815 games, and he played 745 complete games with 7,354 innings total pitched. His pitching award is highly coveted and many Pitchers strive to be like him.

Lefty Grove

Grove is known as the best left-handed Pitcher. Pitchers like him are sought after because their pitches are harder to hit due to the rarity of left-handed players. He had 2,226 career strikeouts, won an MVP award, had eight seasons in which he won 20 games, one season where he won 30 games, and he was the American League earned run average champion nine times.

A pitcher after throwing a pitch.

First Baseman

Lou Gehrig

For 13 straight seasons, Lou Gehrig had more than 100 runs batted in (RBIs) (his hits resulted in his fellow teammates making it to Home Plate and scoring). In 1931, he set the American League record for RBIs at 184. He was a seven-time All-Star, won two MVP awards, and played 2,130 consecutive games, holding the record for most games played for 56 years. Sadly, the reason you've probably heard of this guy is because he contracted and died from amyotrophic lateral sclerosis or ALS, now referred to as 'Lou Gehrig's disease.'

Jimmie Fox

For 12 straight seasons, Fox hit at least 30 Home Runs and more than 100 RBIs. For five of those seasons, he hit at least 40. He was MVP three seasons, ranks ninth of all time for RBIs with 1,922, and was inducted into the Hall of Fame in 1951.

Second Baseman

Rogers Hornsby

Hornsby has the highest career batting average for a right-handed hitter. He has won two MVPs and seven batting awards. He was the first ever player to hit 40 Home Runs in a season for the National League.

Jackie Robinson

Jackie Robinson was the first ever Black player to play in the Major League. He was Rookie of the Year in 1947, an All-Star for six straight seasons from 1949 to 1954. He played for the Dodgers when they won the World Series in 1955 and played in six World Series total. His number, 42, has since been retired by the Dodgers, meaning no other player on that team will ever wear the same number as Robinson. April 15th, the day that Robinson made his debut in the MLB is celebrated across the country and known as "Jackie Robinson" day. On this day, all players in the MLB wear the number "42" to honor Robinson.

Third Baseman

Alex Rodriguez

Nicknamed "A-Rod," Rodriguez has hit 518 Home Runs. He was the quickest player to reach 500 Home Runs. He has won three MVP awards, one batting title, and he has played in 10 All-Star games.

Michael Schmidt

Schmidt hit 548 Home Runs, was a three-time MVP winner, awarded 10 Golden Gloves for his fielding, and won a World Series in 1980.

Shortstop

Honus Wagner

Wagner was an excellent hitter, with 3,145 career hits and eight batting titles. He led the League in stolen bases four times, and was voted into the Hall of Fame during the first vote in 1936.

Left Fielder

Ted Williams

Ted Williams is another well-known hitter, receiving the MVP award twice. He had 512 career Home Runs. He also has been given the title of the "best Left Fielder of all time."

Barry Bonds

Bonds is one of those controversial players, as he was accused of using steroids to enhance his performance in the game. However, with 762 Home Runs and 1,996 RBIs, his stats are impossible to ignore. He also has a record winning seven MVP awards.

Center Fielder

Willie Mays

Mays won the Rookie of the Year award in 1951. In his 22-year career, he led the League in Home Runs four times. He had 660 Home Runs in his career, and he stole 338 bases. He was very fast and an excellent hitter. Defensively, he had an excellent throwing arm and won 12 Golden Glove awards.

Mickey Mantle

Mantle had a whopping seven World Series titles and an excellent batting average. He had 536 Home Runs and 1,509 RBIs in his career, making it to the Home Plate 1,676 times. He was voted MVP three times and made it on the All Star team 20 times.

Right Fielder

Babe Ruth

You've probably heard of this guy. Nicknamed "the Babe," this player led the league in several stats. He won the MVP award several times. He started playing for the Boston Red Sox, but after a poor season he was traded to the New York Yankees (although some believe the trade was made because of monetary reasons). There, he became an icon. Over his 22-season career, he hit 714 Home Runs. There were 12 seasons in which he scored more than 100 runs, 13 seasons where he had more than 100 RBIs, and he was the first player ever to hit 30, 40, 50, and 60 Home Runs in one season. Many people consider Babe Ruth the greatest baseball player of all time, as he could not only hit but he could pitch too! After trading Ruth, the Red Sox did not win a World Series for another 86 years. Many fans refer to this as the "Curse of the Bambino" and consider this to have been punishment for trading one of the best baseball players in history.

Hank Aaron

Aaron broke the record for the most runs scored, at 2,174. He beat none other than Babe Ruth for that record on April 8th, 1974, while playing for the Atlanta Braves. He held the record until it was beaten by Barry Bonds in 2007. He scored 755 Home Runs and had 2,297 RBIs.

Other Outfielders

Ken Griffey Jr.

One outfielder who dominated the 1990s was Ken Griffey Jr. He had a whopping 630 Home Runs and 1,836 RBIs in his career. For much of his career, he was considered the face of baseball.

Rickey Henderson

No one stole more bases on the field than Henderson. He also has a total of 297 career Home Runs, 1,115 RBIs, and a staggering 1,406 stolen bases. He also stole 130 bases in one season, the only person who'd done it.

Designated Hitter

Joe DiMaggio

DiMaggio had 361 career Home Runs, nine seasons in which he had more than 100 RBIs, and only struck out 369 times in his 6,821 career at-bats. He was a three-time MVP award winner and nine-time World Series Champion. He held a record of 56 consecutive games in which he got a hit while at bat. He also played Centerfield.

David Ortiz

"Big Papi" is a 10-time All-Star who played 20 seasons in Major League Baseball. He won three World Series titles with the Boston Red Sox and seven *Silver Slugger* awards for his excellent batting. He set the Red Sox single-season Home Run record when he hit 54 of them in the 2006 season.

Summary

Whoa. Think you might be ready to have an in-depth conversation about the best baseball players with your baseball-loving friend?

If you go up to your friends and mention how you think Ted Williams or Mickey Mantle are some of the greatest outfielders in history, you will likely get an earful on why they agree (or disagree) with you.

You also have the knowledge to talk about records set and broken by Babe Ruth, Hank Aaron, and Barry Bonds.

If you decide to start playing baseball, you now know some of the players who were the best in the position you might play. For example, if you learn to play Catcher, it'll be a treat to watch Yadier Molina play for the Cardinals every season.

Now that we know the best players in each position, let's see what teams are the best in this sport's history.

Chapter 4
The 20 Best Teams of all Time

An old baseball team and their managers.

Remember when I said that Babe Ruth started playing with the Boston Red Sox before he was traded to the Yankees? It wasn't until the Babe was traded that he became the icon he is today. Many superstitious baseball players and fans say that the Red Sox were cursed after they traded baseball's greatest player. They did not win another World Series for 86 years.

Today, the Red Sox are one of the best teams in the game. But which teams hold that title for all of history?

The following is a list of some of the best teams of all time, since the invention of baseball. Of course, baseball history has a lot more to offer than just 20 great teams, but this list is based off of winning records, World Series Championships, best players, and Home Runs, and excellent management according to David Anicetti (2021).

#20. 2002 Oakland Athletics

With a winning record of 103–59, many fans were disappointed when this excellent team lost the American League championship to the Minnesota Twins. The team was on a roll when they won 20 straight games in August and September. Players Eric Chavez and Miguel Tejada hit 34 Home Runs each. Pitcher Jermaine Dye was highly praised for his 24 Home Runs and 86 RBIs that season.

#19. 2001 Seattle Mariners

This team won a total of 116 regular season games in 2001. They were armed with incredible batter Ichiro Suzuki, who had 242 hits that season with 56 stolen bases. Bret Boone hit 37 Home Runs, and Edgar

Martinez hit 106 Home Runs that season. It would have been one of the greatest baseball seasons of all time, but the Mariners failed to win a Series. Sadly, they were eliminated from the American League championships by the New York Yankees.

#18. 2016 Chicago Cubs

After more than a century of failing to win a World Series, the 2016 Cubs started the season ready to make history. They won 103 regular season games. Their players were excellent batters, with Anthony Rizzo and Kris Bryant both hitting 32 Home Runs and more than 100 RBIs. In the World Series against the Cleveland Indians, the Cubs won with four wins over the Indians' three-win lead.

#17. 1972 Oakland Athletics

The "As" make another appearance on our list. This season, they won 93 regular season games and won the World Series over the Cincinnati Reds with a 4–3 lead. They had some of the best Pitchers in the League, with infamous Rollie Fingers closing out many of their games. That year, the team was first in the American League for Home Runs.

#16. 2018 Boston Red Sox

The Red Sox won the World Series over the Dodgers in 2018 with a lead of 4–1. They won 108 regular season games and won the Fall Classic against the Yankees, Astros, and Dodgers. Their defense was some of the best of all time, and their pitching team was excellent.

#15. 1989 Oakland Athletics

And the As are back again! This team had a great season with 99 regular season wins, followed by a World Series shutout (they won enough games and did not let the other team win any). Mark McGuire hit 33 Home Runs that season, with Rickey Henderson stealing 52 bases on his own. The team stole 157 bases all together, and the pitching team was rewarded for allowing the fewest runs scored that season.

#14. 1969 New York Mets

The 69 Mets had an excellent pitching team, winning 100 games in one season. They beat the Orioles in the World Series with four wins and one loss.

#13. 1995 Atlanta Braves

Another team with excellent pitching was the 1995 Braves. Pitcher John Smoltz had a mean knuckleball pitch that was difficult to hit. And if the pitching wasn't enough, they were armed with wonderful hitters, like Chipper Jones and Fred McGriff. They won 90 regular games and won the World Series over the Indians.

#12. 2004 Boston Red Sox

With a winning record of 98–64, the Red Sox also won the World Series this year against the Cardinals. This was the year the Sox finally broke the alleged 'curse' that they got when they traded Babe Ruth to the Yankees. They had Manny Ramirez and David Ortiz on their hitting team, and in total the team scored 949 Home Runs.

#11. 1968 Detroit Tigers

This team had a winning record of 103 wins, and beat the Cardinals in a tight win in the World Series. Their Pitcher Denny McLain won both the Cy Young award and MVP that year. The team hit a total of 185 Home Runs and were first in the American League that year.

#10. 1967 St. Louis Cardinals

Orlando Cepeda won the National League MVP this season, hitting 25 Home Runs. Another Cardinal legend, Lou Brock, hit 21 Home Runs and stole 52 bases. They had an excellent pitcher, Dick Hughes, and they won the World Series against the Red Sox.

#9. 1927 New York Yankees

This team was known for Babe Ruth and Lou Gehrig being on their team and had a batter's lineup nicknamed "Murderer's Row" for their hitting power. This season, the Yankees won 110 regular games, with Ruth hitting 60 Home Runs and 164 RBIs, and Gehrig finishing with 47 Home Runs and 175 RBIs. They won the Series over the Pirates in a 4–0 shutout.

#8. 1976 Cincinnati Reds

This team dominated their season with 106 victorious regular games and won their second consecutive World Series this year. George Foster led the team in Home Runs, hitting 29 the whole season. They also had Johnny Bench (one of the best catchers mentioned in the previous chapter). When they beat the Yankees in the Series, it was a four-game shutout.

#7. 1984 Detroit Tigers

Winning 104 games, the Tigers had a great offense this season. Kirk Gibson hit 27 Home Runs and had 91 RBIs, while Lance Parrish helped with hitting 33 Home Runs. They won the World Series over the Padre, only losing one game. All three of their starting Pitchers won 15 games each.

#6. 1986 New York Mets

This Team led the National League in both hits and Home Runs this season. They had quite a lineup, including Bob Ojeda and Ron Darling. They went on to beat the Red Sox in the World Series.

#5. 1970 Baltimore Orioles

The Orioles started the 1970s with a World Series win against the Reds after winning 108 regular season games. Frank Robinson hit 25 Home Runs and Brooks Robinson finished the season with an excellent batting average and as baseball's best third baseman.

#4. 1975 Cincinnati Reds

Remember when I said the Cincinnati Reds won back-to-back World Series? This team made that possible. This season, the team scored a total of 840 Home Runs. They had one of the most feared batting lineups, including Pete Rose, who had more than 200 hits, and of course, Johnny Bench. They beat the Red Sox in a hard-earned seven-game battle in the World Series.

#3. 1961 New York Yankees

This team was armed with Mickey Mantle, Roger Maris, and Yogi Berra. Maris and Mantle hit 61 and 54 Home Runs, respectively. Pitcher Whitney Ford struck out 209 batters, and the team finished first in Home Runs in the American League. The team beat the Reds in the World Series.

#2. 1939 New York Yankees

It's no surprise that the Yankees are so popular on this list. Many baseball legends have played for them throughout history. This team in particular, won 106 regular games and won the Series in a shutout against the Reds. Joe DiMaggio had 30 Home Runs and 126 RBIs (in a time when Home Runs were difficult to hit). Many players from this team are now Hall of Famers.

#1. 1998 New York Yankees

Remember what I said about the Yankees being special? This team had an excellent batting lineup and an amazing closing Pitcher in Mariano Rivera. In the Playoffs, the team had a record of 11–2 (11 wins and 2 losses), and they won a whopping 114 regular season games before beating the Padres in the World Series with a four-game shutout.

Summary

Wow! What a list. Of course, this is only one list based on specific criteria. Other lists may include different teams, or rank these same teams different. However, you at least have an effective list to speak to your friends and other fans about when the conversation comes up!

Keep in mind that many of the teams listed in this chapter may contain some of the same players that participated in other teams. For example, the Yankees made the list a few times with Babe Ruth and Lou Gehrig in their lineup. However, the teams are ranked the way they are (by year) because players and teams all have their good and bad seasons.

Next, let's explore some of the coaches that make these teams so great!

CHAPTER 5

THE BEST COACHES AND MANAGERS OF ALL TIME

Now that we've learned about the best players and the best teams, let's discuss the coaches. Mostly called *managers* in Major League Baseball, these coaches have been recognized as the best throughout history.

Sadly, managers are largely under-appreciated. Their most important role is setting up the lineup for batting, fielding, and pitching, making in-game decisions such as sending in a new pitcher, and switching out a hitter (called a pinch hitter). Also, one of their most difficult roles is managing the team. Many professional teams have many players, meaning there are many personalities confined in one space. Managers must make sure teammates can get along and play well together.

This list is compiled of 30 managers who performed these roles the best. Many of them have coached multiple World Series Champions, League champions, and excellent winning teams. Many of them are even part of the esteemed Hall of Fame.

#30. Bucky Harris

This man coached several teams throughout the years, including the Washington Senators from 1924 to 1928, again in 1935 to 1942, and a third time in 1950 to 1954. He coached the Detroit Tigers from 1929 to 1933 and again from 1955 to 1956, the Boston Red Sox in 1934, the Philadelphia Phillies in 1943, and the New York Yankees from 1947 to 1948. Harris won the World Series with the Senators in 1924 and with the Yankees in 1947. He was also awarded with three pennants from the American League and was inducted into the Hall of Fame in 1975.

#29. Billy Southworth

Southworth coached the St. Louis Cardinals in 1929 and then again from 1940 to 1945. He coached the Boston Braves (now the Atlanta Braves) from 1946 to 1949, and again from 1950 to 1951. He was awarded four National League pennants and was inducted into the Hall of Fame in 2008. When managing the Cardinals, they won 105 games or more for three seasons and at least 95 wins in two other seasons. He also led the Boston Braves to a winning record five of six seasons, a record at the time for the team. As for his winning average, Southworth placed 12th all time.

#28. Dusty Baker

Baker managed the San Francisco Giants from 1993 to 2002, the Chicago Cubs from 2003 to 2006, the Cincinnati Reds from 2008 to 2013, the Washington Nationals from 2016 to 2017, and the Houston Astros from 2020 to the present. He won the National League Manager of the Year three times, and he won the National League pennant in 2002. He won 840 games in 10 seasons while coaching the Giants. He had 10 seasons in which his team won 90 games or more.

#27. Billy Martin

Martin coached the Minnesota Twins in 1969, the Detroit Tigers from 1971 to 1973, the Texas Rangers from 1973 to 1975, the New York Yankees from 1975 to 1979, again in 1983, 1985, and 1988, and the Oakland Athletics from 1980 to 1982. Martin was a coach who had difficulty getting along with people. After his one season coaching the Twins, he led them to 97 wins in the season, but got into a fight with some players that ended with him being fired. After a year off, he went to the Tigers, where he led the team to three seasons of winning records. Sadly, he was fired from there too in 1973. He went to the Texas Rangers, and during his first and only full season with the team, he led them to a winning record after back-to-back seasons of losing more than 100 games. But then, Martin was fired from the Rangers too due to a clash with the team's ownership. With the Athletics, two of his three seasons were successful, but the third season ended in a losing record-the first for Martin, and he was fired. With the Yankees, he won a World Series and was awarded the American League pennant.

#26. Cito Gaston

Gaston was the manager of the Toronto Blue Jays from 1989 to 1997, then again from 2008 to 2010. He won back-to-back World Series titles in 1992 and 1993 and was awarded two American League pennants. He was the first Black manager to win a World Series title. He started out as a batting coach, a position he held for 7 years before he was promoted. Sadly, after the Blue Jays had four straight seasons with losing records, Gaston was fired as manager. He did remain part of the team as hitting coach. In 2008, he was rehired as the manager and coached for 2 years before he retired after a winning season with the Blue Jays.

#25. Cap Anson

Anson coached the Philadelphia Athletics in 1875, the Chicago White Stockings from 1879 to 1889, the Chicago Colts from 1890 to 1897, and the New York Giants in 1898. He was awarded five National League pennants and inducted into the Hall of Fame in 1939 as a player. His career winning percentage places 13th in history and in the top 10 for coaches with more than 10 years of experience. During his first full season with the White Stockings (who would later become the Cubs), they had an incredible season of 67 wins and only 17 losses. He is also known as one of the best first basemen of all time, and is one of the first great baseball players of all time.

#24. Frank Selee

Selee was the coach of the Boston Beaneaters from 1890 to 1901, the Chicago Orphans in 1902, and the Chicago Cubs from 1903 to 1905. He has five National League pennants and was inducted into the Hall of Fame in 1999. He ranks fourth in career winning percentages. The 1898 Beaneaters (who went on to become the Braves), was the first team in history to win more than 100 games in a season.

#23. Dick Williams

Williams managed the Boston Red Sox from 1967 to 1969, the Oakland Athletics from 1971 to 1973, the California Angels from 1974 to 1976, the Montreal Expos from 1977 to 1981, the San Diego Padres from 1982 to 1985, and the Seattle Mariners from 1986 to 1988. He has two back-to-back World Series titles with the Athletics in 1972 and 1973. Willians has three American League pennants and one National League pennant. He was inducted into the Hall of Fame in 2008. He is one of the most well-traveled coaches in MLB history. Also, while he was with the Athletics, he won 288 games in three seasons. In the 4 years he managed the Padres, the team had no losing records. He retired with 1,571 wins under his belt.

#22. Billy McKechnie

McKechnie coached the Newark Pepper in 1915, the Pittsburgh Pirates from 1922 to 1926, the St. Louis Cardinals from 1928 to 1929, the Boston Braves from 1930 to 1935, Boston Bees from 1936 to 1937, and the Cincinnati Reds from 1938 to 1946. He has two World Series Titles with the Pirates in 1925 and the Reds in 1940. He has four National League pennants and was inducted into the Hall of Fame in 1962. In 1915, he was both a player and a manager for the Newark Pepper, which was part of the Federal League. His Series win with the Pirates was the second in their team's history. However, in 1935 in Boston, his team had a record winning (or losing, depending on how you look at it) 115 losses in one season, despite Babe Ruth being on their team.

#21. Fred Clarke

Clarke was the coach for the Louisville Cardinals from 1897 to 1899 and the Pittsburgh Pirates from 1900 to 1915. He won four National League pennants and a World Series in 1909 with the Pirates. He was inducted into the Hall of Fame as a player in 1945. While McKechnie led the Pirates to their second Series win, it was Clarke who led them to their first. In 1909, the team won 110 games in the regular season, which was the last time the team won more than 100 games in one season.

#20. Jim Leyland

Leyland was the manager of the Pirates from 1986 to 1996, the Florida Marlins from 1997 to 1998, the Colorado Rockies in 1999, and the Detroit Tigers from 2006 to 2013. He won the World Series with the Marlins in 1997 and he won two American League pennants and one National League pennant. He was voted Manager of the Year three times, in 1990, 1992, and 2006. He led the Marlins to their first World Series title. In the 8 years he coached the Tigers, he had a record of 700 wins and 597 losses. He also managed Team USA to a Gold Medal in the 2017 World Baseball Classic.

#19. Davey Johnson

Johnson was the manager of the New York Mets from 1984 to 1990, Cincinnati Reds from 1993 to 1995, Baltimore Orioles from 1996 to 1997, Los Angeles Dodgers from 1999 to 2000, and Washington Nationals from 2011 to 2013. He won the 1986 World Series with the Mets and a National League pennant the same year. His first year with the Mets, they won 90 regular season games, 22 more than their previous season. The following two seasons they won 98 and 108 games, respectively. In 7 years, Johnson's winning percentage was the highest in the team's history. He had similar success with his other teams, only posting one losing record with the Dodgers in 1999.

#18. Al Lopez

Lopez coached the Cleveland Indians from 1951 to 1956 and the Chicago White Stockings from 1957 to 1965 and again from 1968 to 1969. He had two American League Pennants and was inducted into the Hall of Fame in 1977. He ranks ninth in all time winning percentage and fourth in managers with more than 2,000 games experience. His winning percentage with the Cleveland Indians is still the best in the team's history, and never had a losing season in his entire career. He is considered one of the best managers to never win a World Series.

#17. Terry Francona

Francona managed the Philadelphia Phillies from 1997 to 2000, the Boston Red Sox from 2004 to 2011, and the Cleveland Indians from 2013 to the present. He has two World Series titles with the Red Sox in 2004 and 2007, three American League pennants, and has been voted American League Manager of the Year twice, once in 2013 and again in 2016. After four losing seasons with the Phillies, Francona was fired and bounced around a bit before landing a manager position with the Red Sox. He led the team to their first World Series win in 86 years, breaking what many called the "Curse of the Bambino" (Babe Ruth). After his time with the Red Sox, he took a year off and rejoined the League coaching the Indians, where he still coaches today.

#16. Leo Durocher

Durocher was the coach of the Brooklyn Dodgers from 1939 to 1946 and then again in 1948, the New York Giants from 1948 to 1955, the Chicago Cubs from 1966 to 1972, and the Houston Astros from 1972 to 1973. He won the 1954 World Series with the Giants, three National League pennants, and was inducted into the Hall of Fame in 1994. He started out as a player/manager, and won some Series titles with the New York Yankees and the St. Louis Cardinals. He played with the Dodgers and led them to two 100-game winning seasons before he became a full-time manager.

#15. Jim Mutrie

Mutrie was the coach of the New York Metropolitans from 1883 to 1884 and the New York Giants from 1885 to 1891. He won two World Series titles with the Giants in 1888 and 1889. He had eight winning records in his managerial career and is known for changing the Giants names to the Gotham's.

#14. Frank Chance

Chance coached the Chicago Cubs from 1905 to 1912, the New York Yankees from 1913 to 1914, and the Boston Red Sox in 1923. He won two World Series titles with the Cubs in 1907 and 1908, four National League pennants, and was inducted into the Hall of Fame in 1946 as a player. He was a player/manager for the Cubs during their most successful period in history.

He had a great winning percentage with the Cubs but was less successful in New York and Boston.

#13. Bruce Bochy

Bochy was coach of the San Diego Padres from 1995 to 2006 and the San Francisco Giants from 2007 to 2019. He won three World Series titles with the Giants in 2010, 2012, and 2014. He also won four National League pennants and was voted Manager of the Year in 1996. With the Padres, he had three straight winning seasons from 2004 to 2006. Bochy's first two seasons with the Giants were losing ones, but after that the team turned around. They won 88 wins in 2009, and that was the beginning of one of the most successful winning runs in the team's history. When they won the Series in 2010, it was the first title the Giants had won since they moved from New York. He is one of only 10 managers with three World Series wins in MLB history.

#12. Tommy Losorda

Losorda coached the Los Angeles Dodgers from 1976 to 1996. He won two World Series titles in 1981 and 1988, four National League pennants, was voted Manager of the Year in 1983 and 1988, and was inducted into the Hall of Fame in 1997. He started out as a Pitcher, though he did not have great success. When he became a manager though, his career picked up. When the Dodgers won the Series in 1981, it was their first win since 1965. He also managed Team USA to a gold medal in the 2000 Summer Olympics.

#11. Miller Huggins

Huggins coached the St. Louis Cardinals from 1913 to 1917 and the New York Yankees from 1918 to 1929. He won three World Series titles with the Yankees in 1923, 1927, and 1928, six American League pennants, and was inducted into the Hall of Fame in 1964. Huggins led the Yankees to their first ever Series win. He coached both Babe Ruth and Lou Gehrig, who was only 19 years old when he joined. He coached what many call the best lineup in baseball history.

#10. Water Alston

Alston coached the Brooklyn Dodgers 1954 to 1957 and followed them to Los Angeles and coached them from 1958 to 1976. He has four World Series titles in 1955, 1959, 1963, and 1965, seven National League pennants, and was inducted into the Hall of Fame in 1983. In his 23 years with the Dodgers, Alston won 2,040 games, ranking ninth on the all time list (when he retired, it ranked number five).

#9. Connie Mack

Mack coached the Pittsburgh Pirates from 1894 to 1896 and the Philadelphia Athletics from 1901 to 1950. He has five World Series titles from 1910, 1911, 1913, 1929, and 1930 with the Athletics. He won nine American League pennants and was inducted into the

Hall of Fame in 1937. He holds several Major League records. Mack won 3,731, which is 1,000 more than the second coach John McGraw. He also lost 3,948, which is 1,500 more than the second coach Tony La Russa. He managed for 53 years, 20 years more than the second and third coach on the list. He managed the Athletics in the first 50 years of the team's existence and was even a partial owner.

#8. Bobby Cox

Cox coached the Atlanta Braves from 1978 to 1981 and again from 1990 to 2010. He also coached the Toronto Blue Jays from 1982 to 1985. He won the 1995 World Series with the Braves, five National League pennants, and was inducted into the Hall of Fame in 2014. He was also voted Manager of the Year four times, once in the American League in 1985, and three times in the National League in 1991, 2004, and 2005. He was ejected from 158 games by the umpire, the most of any coach in MLB history. He is the only manager to be thrown from two World Series games. When he returned to the Braves in 1990, he turned the team around. They had placed last in their division the previous season, but they won 94 games under Cox's leadership. They had several seasons in which they won more than 100 games while under Cox's management.

#7. Earl Weaver

Weaver coached the Baltimore Orioles from 1968 to 1982, and again from 1985 to 1986. He won the World Series in 1970 as well as four American League pennants. He was inducted into the Hall of Fame in 1996. He won 1,480 games in his 17 seasons with the Orioles. His winning average ranks 10th on the leaderboard and his postseason wins rank 15th. He was well known for fighting with umpires, getting thrown out of more than 90 games.

#6. Tony La Russa

La Russa coached the Chicago White Sox from 1979 to 1986, the Oakland Athletics from 1986 to 1995, and the St. Louis Cardinals from 1996 to 2011. He won three World Series, with the Athletics in 1989 and with the Cardinals in 2006 and 2011. He has three American League pennants and three National League pennants. He was voted Manager of the Year four times and was inducted into the Hall of Fame in 2014. La Russa took the Cardinals to the World Series for the first time in 2004, though they lost to the Red Sox. He ranks number three on the all time wins list for the MLB.

#5. Joe Torre

Torre coached the New York Mets from 1977 to 1981, Atlanta Braves from 1982 to 1984, St. Louis Cardinals from 1990 to 1995, New York Yankees from 1996 to 2007, and the Los Angeles Dodgers from 2008 to 2010. He won four World Series titles, six American League pennants, Manager of the Year twice, and was inducted into the Hall of Fame in 2014. In his 3 years with the Braves, he won 257 games. His first season with the Yankees, he led the team to their first World championship in 18 years. He won three back-to-back World Series titles. Torre retired with 2,326 wins, ranking fifth of all time.

#4. Sparky Anderson

Anderson was manager of the Cincinnati Reds from 1970 to 1978 and the Detroit Tigers from 1979 to 1995. He has three World Series titles, four National League pennants, one American League pennant, was voted Manager of the Year twice, and was inducted into the Hall of Fame in 2000. His first season with the Reds was successful, leading them from third place to playing in the World Series, though they lost to the Orioles that year. When he won the Series in 1984, he was the first manager ever to win it in both the American and National League. He retired with 2,194 wins.

#3. Casey Stengel

Stengel coached the Brooklyn Dodgers from 1934 to 1936, the Boston Bees from 1938 to 1940, Boston Braves from 1941 to 1943, the New York Yankees from 1949 to 1960, and the New York Mets from 1962 to 1965. He won a whopping seven World Series titles and 10 American League pennants. He was inducted into the Hall of Fame in 1966. In his first nine seasons between Brooklyn and Boston, Stengel only had one winning season in 1938. Then, in his first five seasons with the Yankees, they won five back-to-back World Series titles, setting the record for consecutive world titles. He never had a losing season with the Yankees in 12 years. He had less success when he went to the Mets, and retired after a few losing seasons with them.

#2. John McGraw

McGraw coached the Baltimore Orioles in 1899, again from 1901 to 1902, and the New York Giants 1902 to 1932. He won three World Series titles, 10 National League pennants, and 2,763 games. He was inducted into the Hall of Fame in 1937. McGraw held the record for most wins until Connie Mack broke it in 1984. His 10 pennants tie with Stengel for the most in Major League history. His first eight seasons as a manager, he was also an excellent player. His entire career, he only had two losing seasons. McGraw won back to back World Series in 1921 and 1922. He was the second manager in history to win three World Series. He ranks 10th all time for games won.

#1. Joe McCarthy

McCarthy was the coach of the Chicago Cubs from 1926 to 1930, the New York Yankees from 1931 to 1946, and the Boston Red Sox from 1948 to 1950. He won seven World Series titles, all with the Yankees. He has eight American League pennants and one National League pennant. He was inducted into the Hall of

Fame in 1957. He won those seven World titles in 16 seasons. He never had a losing season with the Yankees in all 16 years. In fact, in 24 years as a manager, McCarthy had no losing seasons. He was the first manager to win a pennant in both the National and American Leagues. He coached Babe Ruth, Lou Gehrig, and Ted Williams. His career 2,125 wins ranks eighth of all time, though it stood at fifth when he ranked. He has the best winning record in MLB history.

Summary

Wow! Thirty coaches, so many World Series wins! And all those pennants! Who knew how important a coach could be to a team, especially a professional one!

With the last chapter, you now have an impressive amount of knowledge to share with your peers. Not only can you talk about players, but coaches too!

Unfortunately, many people don't know how important the role of the manager is. Some don't even know the responsibilities of Major League managers. Coaching is different in the Major League than it is at your local school or for your community baseball team.

It's also important to note that for professional teams, the manager is not the only coach. Rather, they are in charge of several coaches, such as base coaches, pitching coaches, and batting coaches.

Base coaches watch the ball while it is in play, so the runners can focus on getting to the base. They are usually positioned at First and Third Base. They use signals and even words to tell runners whether they should stop at a base or run to the next one.

Pitching coaches are exactly what they sound like. They are in charge of working with the Pitchers to better their throwing. They also help the Pitchers get warmed up before they are put on the field.

Batting coaches are those in charge of helping players get better at hitting. They practice with players to keep them good at their jobs.

Finally, like the chapter before, the previous list is one list based on specific criteria. Other lists may rank managers differently or even name totally different people.

Now that we've talked about players, teams, and coaches that set some amazing records, let's talk about those records in depth and why they're so amazing.

Chapter 6
Best Records and Fun Facts

There are lots of records set by amazing players, teams, and managers throughout baseball history. Many of these are set by the players we talked about in Chapter 3 and the managers in Chapter 5. Some of these records are considered 'unbreakable.' Others say records are meant to be broken. Let's explore these records and compare.

Best Records

Let's start with the records set throughout history before we dive into the fun facts. We can begin by listing the top five records that are considered by many to be unbreakable.

Top Five Unbreakable Records in Baseball

1. Consecutive Games Played

This record was set by Cal Ripken Jr. when he played 2,632 consecutive baseball games. Previously, the record had been set by Lou Gehrig, who held the title with 2,131 games played. The sheer amount of games played by these two individuals is astonishing, considering the toll it must have taken on them physically. The closest to either of these records anyone else has gotten was Miguel Tejada, whose streak reached 1,152 before it ended in 2007.

2. Career Batting Average

Ty Cobb not only has the highest batting average (he has more hits than strikeouts), but he had that batting average for five straight seasons. In order for anyone to even attempt to break this record, a batter would need more than 3,000 at-bats (and they would need to be successful every time).

3. Career Strikeouts

This record was set by Nolan Ryan with 5,714 strikeouts. With most Pitchers today only lasting for about six to seven innings each game, their ability to reach that number is severely impaired. The two Pitchers behind Ryan on the list, Roger Clemens and Randy Johnson, are both thousands of strikeouts behind the record.

4. Hit Streak

Joe DiMaggio holds this record with a 56-game streak in which he hit a ball every game. Only 43 players have had a hit for 30 or more consecutive games. Jimmy Rollins is the only one who came close when he had a 38-game hitting streak, but no one has come any closer to breaking DiMaggio's record.

5. On-Base Plus Slugging (OPS) Percentage

Babe Ruth had a higher combination of Home Runs and times on base than any other player. He holds that record with a percentage of 1.546. The next closest player is Barry Bonds, with an OPS of 1.421, more than 100 points behind Ruth.

Other Records

Career Hits

This record belongs to Pete Rose, with 4,256 hits in his whole career. Ty Cobb, our record holder for the best batting average, is the only other player in history besides Rose who had more than 4,000 hits in their career, but though Rose's batting average was lower than that of Cobb's, Rose holds the record for most hits (*Top 10 unbreakable baseball records*, 2018).

Games Won

With 511 wins across five teams and 21 years of baseball, this record belongs to history pitcher Cy Young. The leader of the modern era is Warren Spaghn, but he is still 147 wins behind Young. Second place during Young's time belonged to Walter Johnson, who trailed behind Young with 416 wins in his career (which is still an incredible career).

Season Wins

The most games won in a season by one player was 59, and that record belongs to Charles "Old Hoss" Radbourn. Radbourn set this record a whopping 134 years ago and the record has yet to be broken.

Most RBIs in One Season

Remember, RBIs are when a batter hits a ball that results in their fellow teammates making it to Home and scoring. The most RBIs hit by one player in one season is 191, and that record belongs to Hack Wilson. Thanks to him, 191 players on base made it to Home off his at-bat in one season. This record becomes harder to break as more and more excellent batters join baseball, and it's getting to where there are more Home Runs than RBIs.

Back-to-Back No Hitters

A no-hitter means that a Pitcher throws a perfect game. In other words, no ball thrown by the Pitcher is hit by a batter, and no players are walked to their base. A no-hitter game has only happened 299 times in Major League Baseball history, only 34 players have ever done it more than once, and the only person who's ever done it twice in a row is Johnny Vander Meer. For anyone to beat that record, a Pitcher would have to throw 27 straight innings without a ball being hit by a batter.

Stolen Bases

Stealing bases is hard. You have to be fast and pick your moment. You can't get caught by the Pitcher or the fielder guarding the base you're trying to steal. So, that makes the record of 1,406 stolen bases pretty impressive, and that record is held by Rickey Henderson. As time goes on, the number of players stealing bases goes down, making this record even more difficult to break.

Manager Records

Players aren't the only ones who get to set records. The managers who led so many teams to victory are also ranked with some pretty awesome stats.

All Time Wins (and Losses)

The record for most regular season games won belongs to Connie Mack, who also holds the record for most games lost. With 3,731 wins and 3,938 losses, Mack's record in both will be difficult to break. Second place for wins is Tony LaRussa, with only 2,821 wins.

Winning Average

This record belongs to Dave Roberts, who has managed 872 games. Of those, he had a record of 542 wins and 330 losses, earning him a winning average of .622 and setting the record. Just behind him is Joe McCarthy, who won 2,125 and lost 1,333 of his 3,487 games played. He has a winning average of .615.

Ejected Games

If you look up coaches fighting with umpires, a picture of Bobbie Cox is likely to pop up in a few minutes. Cox was thrown out of more games than any other coach in MLB history, a whopping 158 times. Coming in second would be Earl Weaver, who was thrown out of more than 90 games.

Fun Facts

Colorado Rockies Mascot

After all we've talked about, what else can we possibly have to do? Why, learn more cool stuff! The great thing about baseball is that, despite how old it is, it is ever changing. While the rules are virtually the same as when they started, players and managers and technology are constantly making the game more interesting, and adaptations are always happening so the game is more entertaining for fans.

So, let's see some cool things to know, so you can share these the next time your friends are talking about baseball and you want to join in!

- ⊃ For example, did you know a baseball game in the Major League usually lasts about 3 hours? That's right. You should have lots of patience when watching a game, especially if you are outside. The sheer length of professional games led to the birth of the 'seventh inning stretch,' in which the game pauses for a few minutes and the fans get up and stretch to fun music in the stadium.

- ⊃ Another fact is that a regular baseball season has a whopping 162 games. Remember how close some of those teams in Chapter 4 got to that number? That's a lot of games to play such a physically taxing sport.

- ⊃ Remember all the coaches and players that made the Hall of Fame? There's a lot of esteemed baseball members that have been inducted. The team with the honor of having the most in the Hall of Fame is the Yankees, claiming an impressive 27 members.

- ⊃ You may notice your friends or family members that enjoy baseball, getting excited in the springtime. That's because the MLB season starts up in April and goes all through the summer until the end of September. The World Series usually takes place in October. Some teams even sell tickets to Spring Training games just because fans are itching to watch their favorite sport.

- Furthermore, did you know that baseball has been on television since 1939? The first game was a doubleheader (two games played back-to-back) between Cincinnati and Brooklyn on August 26 of that year.

- If you ever go to a baseball stadium and get hungry, make sure to try a hot dog! They're the most popular food item in baseball stadiums. Of course, if hot dogs aren't for you, almost all stadiums have plenty of other snacks and drinks to offer during the game.

Concession stand at a baseball stadium.

◯ Sadly, another fact is that there have been no Major League Baseball games where a female player was on the field. However, as we discussed in Chapter 2, the Women's League was very popular during World War II when many men were off fighting.

- Many baseball players in the major leagues make lots of money. The player with the most money to date is Alex Rodriguez, with $450 million in earnings (Andreajn, 2021).

- The oldest baseball stadium in the world is Labatt Park in London, Ontario Canada, built in 1877.

- The team that's won the most in the Olympics is the Cuban team, who earned their third gold medal in 2004.

- Effa Louise Manley, an American Sports executive, is the first and only woman who was inducted into the baseball Hall of Fame. She co-owned (with her husband) the Newark Eagles baseball team in the Negro Leagues from 1935 to 1948.

- If you've ever heard the song "Take Me Out to the Ballgame" you've probably watched a baseball game or two. It's the unofficial anthem for baseball, and another fun activity for fans to participate in at professional games.

- The longest Major League Baseball game lasted for 8 hours and 6 minutes in 1984, between the Chicago White Sox and the Milwaukee Brewers.

- On the other hand, the shortest professional game recorded was only 31 minutes long. The game started a bit earlier than scheduled, and was finished before the original scheduled start time.

- The game with the most innings ever played was played in 1920, where the Brooklyn Robins and Boston Braves played 26 long innings. The game would have gone on longer if it hadn't gotten dark and the umpires called the game.

- Baseball can be a great father–son activity. The first father-son duo in the MLB was Ken Griffey Sr. and Ken Griffey Jr. They were the first father–son teammates, and they played for the Mariners in 1990.

- Major League Baseball has not had a left-handed Catcher since 1989. They are actually excluded from the position because being left-handed gives them an advantage to throw to Third Base. However, left-handed Pitchers are widely desired due to their ability to throw a ball that is more difficult to hit.

- The fastest pitch ever thrown was 105.1 miles per hour, and it was thrown by Cuban Pitcher Aroldis Chapman in 2010 (Andreajn, 2021).

- The most expensive baseball card ever sold was bought for $3.12 million and features player Honus Wagner. It is so expensive due to being so rare, with only 25 to 200 released cards (Andreajn, 2021). At the time it was first released, the cards were given away in cigarette packs. For some unknown reason, Wagner asked that this was stopped. This led to the card no longer being produced.

- A batter named Richie Ashburn hit two fall balls in a row, and hit the same woman twice. The first broke her nose and the second struck her while the paramedics were carrying her away (Andreajn, 2021). Hopefully, the unlucky woman got to keep both foul balls as souvenirs!

- All Major League baseballs are made of the same materials, and they all have exactly 108 stitches.

- The first baseball caps were worn by the New York Knickerbockers in 1849, and they were made out of straw. Caps nowadays sport the player's team logo.

- When the playoffs begin to determine which teams will go to the World Series, there are 10 teams total that vie for a position in the World championship.

- Presidents of the United States often throw the ceremonial first pitch of the first game of every season. The first president ever to do this was President William Howard Taft in 1910. Presidents have thrown the first pitch ever since, with Jimmy Carter being the exception.

- Remember how we said players wear numbers on their backs? The first team to ever do this was the New York Yankees in the 1920s.

- Finally, baseball has been known as the American pastime since the end of the Civil War.

Summary

Whoa. So many records, set by so many people. And so many cool things surrounding baseball!

If any of these chapters give you the most information to talk with your friends about, it's this one. Remember these quick facts and records to keep up in a conversation about baseball. You'll likely learn even more from your peers!

Like I said before, there is always more to learn with baseball. It will continue changing, even when cars fly and robots can play, too. It has been an American favorite since just after its birth, and I don't see it losing popularity any time soon.

Chapter 7

Baseball Around the World

Baseball has been known as the American pastime since the Civil War, but what about other countries? It is an American invention; however, it was inspired by older European games. We've talked about baseball teams like the Toronto Blue Jays and how the fastest pitch was thrown by a Cuban pitcher, but just how popular is baseball in places around the world? What follows, from *Popularity of baseball around the world*, by Topend Sports (n.d.), is a tour of baseball's influence around the world.

Central/South America

Canada lays claim to a few professional teams, one of which, the Toronto Blue Jays, plays with many American teams in the MLB.

However, Central America has quite a presence in baseball. The Dominican Republic, Puerto Rico, Cuba, and Panama all claim popular baseball teams. They even play against each other. Additionally, many players in the MLB have traveled from some of these places to play with the American teams. These countries usually participate in the sport during the Olympics.

Other South American countries where baseball is popular include Chile, Argentina, Peru, Ecuador, Brazil, Portugal, El Salvador, Panama, Venezuela, Costa Rica, Honduras, and Mexico.

Europe

The games that inspired baseball hailed from Europe, but baseball crossed the ocean to rejoin its roots. The United Kingdom, Ireland, Hungary, Germany, and The Netherlands all have a baseball following. Baseball is also popular in Italy, Denmark, Sweden, Norway, Finland, Austria, Croatia, Switzerland, France, Belgium, and Spain.

There are more followings in Middle Eastern countries such as Iraq, Afghanistan, Kuwait, Pakistan, and the United Arab Emirates.

Asia

As far as the list of baseball popularity around the world goes, China ranks last on the list. Yet, there are even baseball teams there, playing the beloved game.

Ranking above China are Asian countries like South Korea, India, Malaysia, Vietnam, Thailand, Indonesia, Singapore, and the Philippines.

Australia

Baseball has even made it all the way around the world to Australia and New Zealand. These two countries rank 11th and 15th on the popularity list, respectively.

Africa

The only African country that ranks on the popularity list, sitting at number 27, is South Africa.

Summary

There are lots of countries that have a baseball following around the world. The sport is beloved by many and played by more. The Olympics have hosted these worldwide teams before so that they get a chance to compete against each other in the game.

Other than the United States, it would seem that Central and South American countries take the lead on the most baseball popularity.

This list only contains some of the top 75 countries that have a significant baseball popularity. There are likely hundreds of countries with teams and players of the game, and American baseball players come from all around the world as well.

Chapter 8

Major League Teams

We've talked a lot about the Major League, and talked about several of the teams that play for it. We've talked about the oldest ones and the best ones.

But there are a lot of teams we haven't discussed in the Major League. I want to use this chapter to break down the Major League teams so you know who's who.

Teams

There are 30 teams in Major League Baseball: 29 of those teams are American teams, with 1 team (the Toronto Blue Jays) located in Canada.

As I mentioned earlier, teams are grouped into two different leagues: American League and National League. The National League and the American League both have 15 teams.

National League Teams

The 15 teams in the National League are:

1. Arizona Diamondbacks
2. Atlanta Braves
3. Chicago Cubs
4. Cincinnati Reds
5. Colorado Rockies
6. Los Angeles Dodgers
7. Miami Marlins
8. Milwaukee Brewers
9. New York Mets
10. Philadelphia Phillies
11. Pittsburgh Pirates
12. San Diego Padres
13. San Francisco Giants
14. St. Louis Cardinals
15. Washington Nationals

American League Teams

The 15 teams in the American League are:

1. Baltimore Orioles
2. Boston Red Sox
3. Chicago White Sox
4. Cleveland Indians
5. Detroit Tigers
6. Houston Astros
7. Kansas City Royals
8. Los Angeles Angels
9. Minnesota Twins

10. New York Yankees
11. Oakland Athletics
12. Seattle Mariners
13. Tampa Bay Rays
14. Texas Rangers
15. Toronto Blue Jays

These teams play each other within their own league, with the exception of occasional inter-league games. They compete to earn their place in the World Series, where either a National League or an American League team will be crowned champion of the year.

Team Fields

A baseball stadium before a game.

Another exciting fact about MLB is the names of each stadium where the teams play. Of course, these teams we listed travel all around the country to play each other, but they all have a home field. You may hear people say things about a team having a *home field advantage*. That is because teams practice on their home field, and the players know it better than any other field. On the other hand, the visiting team will not know the field as well.

List of MLB Stadiums

Wrigley Field, Chicago, Illinois

This list is each MLB stadium for each team. The name of the team who plays there is next to the stadium name.

1. Angel Stadium (Los Angeles Angels)
2. Busch Stadium (St. Louis Cardinals)
3. Chase Field (Arizona Diamondbacks)
4. Citi Fields (New York Mets)
5. Citizens Bank Park (Philadelphia Phillies)

6. Comerica Park (Detroit Tigers)
7. Coors Field (Colorado Rockies)
8. Dodger Stadium (Los Angeles Dodgers)
9. Fenway Park (Boston Red Sox)
10. Globe Life Field Field (Texas Rangers)
11. Great American Ball Park (Cincinnati Reds)
12. Guaranteed Rate Field (Chicago White Sox)
13. Nationals Park (Washington Nationals)
14. Kauffman Stadium (Kansas City Royals)
15. Marlins Park (Miami Marlins)
16. Miller Park (Milwaukee Brewers)
17. MinuteMaid Park (Houston Astros)
18. Oracle Park (San Francisco Giants)
19. Oriole Park at Camden Yards (Baltimore Orioles)
20. Petco Park (San Diego Padres)
21. PNC Park (Pittsburgh Pirates)
22. Progressive Field (Cleveland Indians)
23. RingCentral Coliseum (Oakland Athletics)
24. Rogers Park (Toronto Blue Jays)
25. SunTrust Park (Atlanta Braves)
26. Target Field (Minnesota Twins)
27. T-Mobile Stadium (Seattle Mariners)
28. Tropicana Field (Tampa Bay Rays)
29. Wrigley Field (Chicago Cubs)
30. Yankee Stadium (New York Yankees)

Fenway Park, Boston, Massachusetts

Summary

There are lots of cool things about Major League Baseball. We discussed several of those fun facts in Chapter 6. Most stadiums do not feature a roof, but there are six of them that have a retractable roof (one that closes or opens depending on weather), and one stadium with a fixed roof.

Eight States have more than one MLB team. Those states are California, Florida, Illinois, New York, Ohio, Pennsylvania, Missouri, and Texas. California has the most, with five teams of its own, including the Los Angeles Angels, Los Angeles Dodgers, San Diego Padres, San Francisco Giants, Oakland Athletics.

The oldest park in the MLB is Fenway Park in Boston, Massachusetts, and the newest is Globe Life

Field in Arlington, Texas. The largest stadium is Dodger Stadium in Los Angeles, California, while the smallest is Tropicana Field in Tampa, Florida.

Chapter 9

Minor League Baseball

Major League Baseball has dominated most of our previous chapters. However, I'd be remiss to avoid talking about Minor League baseball teams. They are an important part in the professional baseball path and have been the starting point for many of baseball's most famous players.

What Is Minor League Baseball?

Minor League Baseball, or MiLB, is a league of professional baseball teams associated with the Major League. Every MiLB team is contracted to a Major League team. The teams are used for player development, giving professional experience to players who may not be ready for the Major League just yet.

MiLB is divided into tiers, with AAA (Triple A) teams being the highest tier before the Major League teams.

Almost every Major League player started in the Minor League and worked their way up. Some of them may have skipped a tier or two on their way up; however, it is also common for Major League teams to send players back to the Minor League if they are young or need to heal from an injury. It is very rare for a player to go straight to the MLB out of high school or college.

If you wanted to join a professional baseball team, your best chance to get *drafted* or chosen by a Minor League team out of high school or college. It is possible for you to try out directly for a Major League team, but again, making it is incredibly rare. There are only 23 players who have gone straight to the MLB without stopping in the Minor Leagues. These players are:

- *Garrett Crochet*: Crochet is a left-handed Pitcher drafted by the Chicago White Sox in the first round in 2020. He was taken straight to the MLB due to the MiLB not having a 2020 season due to the Covid-19 pandemic. At 21 years old, he was the youngest player to ever pitch in the major leagues for the White Sox since 2000.

- *Mike Leake*: Leake is a right-handed Pitcher who was drafted by the Reds in the first round in 2009. He had an excellent career in college at Arizona State University. He was signed to a Minor League, but he never pitched a game in the first season, and then he made the Reds during Spring Training in 2010.

- *Xavier Nady*: Nady is a First Baseman and Outfielder who was selected by the Padres in the second round in 2000. He had an excellent career in college at the University of California, Berkeley, with several awards and a great batting average. He went straight to San Diego and made his MLB debut in September of 2000.

- *Ariel Prieto*: Prieto is a right-handed Pitcher who was chosen by the Athletics in 1995 in the first round of the draft after his college career at Fajardo University in Cuba. He started in Cuba at only 15 years old. He made his debut in July of 1995 with the Athletics.

- *Darren Dreifort*: Dreifort is a right-handed Pitcher that the Dodgers selected in the first round of the draft in 1993. He was the second person chosen for the Dodgers that year, behind none other than Alex Rodriguez. He had awards from his time playing in college at Wichita State University and went straight to Los Angeles.

- *John Olerud*: Olerud is a First Baseman who was chosen by the Blue Jays in the draft's third round in 1989. He played for his college, Washington State University, where he had a great batting average and even pitched a bit. He had quite the success in the MLB, he retired after 17 seasons with three Golden Gloves, two All-Star appearances, and more than 2,200 hits.

- *Jim Abbott:* Abbot was a left-handed Pitcher who inspired fans everywhere when he joined the MLB. He was born without a right hand, but that didn't stop him from being on the field. He was selected by the Angels in 1988 in the first round of the draft after a great career playing for the University of Michigan. He was eventually traded to the Yankees and threw a no-hitter against the Indians in 1993.

- *Pete Incaviglia:* Incaviglia is an Outfielder who was chosen by the Expos in 1985. He was well known in college for his hitting ability, and he was chosen in the first round of the draft. He was later traded to the Rangers. He hit 30 Home Runs in his rookie season and hit more than 20 in the next four seasons.

- *Bob Horner:* Horner was chosen as a Third Baseman by the Braves in the first round of the 1978 draft. He was playing for the Braves just 10 days after he signed with them. He won the National League Rookie of the Year award that year, and hit 23 homers in the half season he got to play.

- *Mike Morgan:* Morgan is a right-handed Pitcher who was chosen by the Athletics in 1978. They drafted him directly out of high school, a rarity. He was only 18 years old when he pitched against the Baltimore Orioles for an entire game.

- *Tim Conroy*: Conroy is a left-handed Pitcher who was drafted in the first round of 1978 by the Athletics. He was also chosen directly from High School. Conroy, also 18, was younger than Morgan by a few months.

- *Brian Milner*: Milner is a Catcher. He was drafted by the Blue Jays in the seventh round in 1978. He was the third player that year to be chosen out of high school. He is the first and only Catcher who has skipped the Minor Leagues. He didn't have a lot of success in the MLB though, and was sent back to the Rookie League, but he never made it back to the Major League.

- *Denny Walling*: Walling is an Outfielder who was chosen by the Athletics in the first round in 1975. He actually was selected by the Giants directly out of high school in 1974, but he went to college at Clemson University. It went well for him, making him more popular in the next draft. He made his debut in the MLB in September 1975 before he was sent back down to the Double A tier in the Minor League.

- *Dick Ruthaven:* A right-handed Pitcher, Ruthaven was selected in the first round of the draft in 1973 by the Phillies. He finished his rookie year with a pretty successful pitching average and a batting average. He stayed in the Major League for 14 years.

- *David Clyde:* Left-handed Pitcher Clyde was selected in the first round of the 1973 draft by the Rangers, directly out of high school. He was sent straight to the Major Leagues to draw in fans, with the intention of being sent back down to the Minor League after a few games. However, Clyde was successful enough that he actually stayed in the MLB.

- *Dave Winfield:* Winfield is an Outfielder chosen by the Padres in the first round of the draft in 1973. He was incredibly athletic, with a great career at the University of Minnesota. He was the first person in history to be drafted by four different professional sports leagues: the National Football League, MLB, National Basketball Association, and the American Basketball Association.

- *Eddie Bane:* Left-handed Pitcher Bane was drafted in the first round of 1973 by the Twins after playing baseball for his college team at Arizona State University. He was sent down the Triple A team before being brought back up to the Twins, but ended up getting sent back to the MiLB and retiring after a shoulder injury.

- *Dave Roberts*: Dave Roberts was the fastest player ever to go from the draft to the Major League. He was chosen by the Padres in the first round in 1972 and made his debut in just over 24 hours later. He played Third Baseman and Catcher, and he had excellent batting success.

- *Pete Broberg*: Broberg is a right-handed Pitcher who was drafted by the Senators in 1971. He spent some time in Montreal and went to Texas with the Expos before they went to Texas to become the Rangers. He was sent back to the Minors after 1974.

- *Burt Hooton*: Hooton was chosen by the Cubs in 1971. He was a right-handed Pitcher that was originally picked by the Mets, but he didn't sign and decided to go to college before coming back and signing with Chicago. He was sent back to Triple A before being traded to the Dodgers in 1975.

- *Rob Ellis*: Third Baseman and Outfielder Ellis was drafted in the first round in 1971 by the Brewers. He was originally chosen in 1968 by the Giants, but he chose to go to college at Michigan State before coming back to be picked by the Brewers. His debut started well but quickly went downhill, and he only played 36 games.

- *Steve Dunning*: Dunning is a right-handed Pitcher who was chosen by the Indians in 1970. Though he had fair success for the Indians in his first season, he was sent down to Triple A his second, but called back halfway through. He was traded to the Rangers, the first of five trades in a 4-year span.

- *Mike Adamson*: Adamson was a right-handed pitcher drafted by the Orioles in 1967. He was the first draft pick to debut in the MLB, skipping the minor league. After playing a few games in Baltimore, he was sent back down to Triple A before being called back again, where he had less success. He was sent back to the MiLB, and never did come back to the Major League.

Minor League Tiers

The highest tier in MiLB is the Triple A team. This tier is where players are most often called up to the parent MLB team.

The second tier is the Double A team, followed by the Class A Advanced or 'High A.' The fourth tier is Class A, also known as 'Low A.' The fifth is the Class A Short Season, or just the 'Short Season', and the final are the two rookie ball teams. They usually play against each other.

There is also a spring training team that plays a few practice games, but they are not considered an official team.

Minor League Salaries

Most Major League players make a lot of money, somewhere in the millions. In the Minor Leagues, however, players make significantly less.

Depending on the tier a player is in, they can earn between $20,000 and $67,000 a year. This is a pretty average salary. A few people in the Minor Leagues make Major League money, but not very many. Triple A team players make about $2,000 to $2,500 a month (Bernier, n.d.).

Once a player is drafted into the Minor Leagues, they are usually contracted for seven seasons to play in the MiLB, unless they sign a contract with the MLB before the end of those seven seasons

Sometimes Minor League players sign a Major League contract and then get sent back down to the Triple A team. These are usually the Minor League players you see making millions of dollars.

MiLB Team Owners

Each Minor League team is independently owned, but the players are actually employed by the parent team organization.

For example, the Triple A Minor League team for the St. Louis Cardinals are the Memphis Redbirds. The Redbirds team is not owned by the Cardinals, but independently owned. However, the Redbirds players are not employed by that owner, rather they are employed by the St. Louis Cardinals organization.

Minor League Teams

There are 120 Minor League baseball teams, spanning the United States, Canada, and the Dominican Republic.

Triple A Teams

These teams are the triple A teams and the Major League teams with which they are affiliated: .

1. Albuquerque Isotopes (Colorado Rockies)
2. Buffalo Bisons (Toronto Blue Jays)
3. Charlotte Knights (Chicago White Sox)
4. Columbus Clippers (Cleveland Indians)
5. Durham Bulls (Tampa Bay Rays)
6. El Paso Chihuahuas (San Diego Padres)
7. Gwinnett Stripers (Atlanta Braves)
8. Indianapolis Indians (Pittsburgh Pirates)
9. Iowa Cubs (Chicago Cubs)

10. Jacksonville Jumbo Shrimp (Miami Marlins)
11. Las Vegas Aviators (Oakland Athletics)
12. LeHigh Valley IronPigs (Philadelphia Phillies)
13. Louisville Bats (Cincinnati Reds)
14. Memphis Redbirds (St. Louis Cardinals)
15. Nashville Sounds (Milwaukee Brewers)
16. Norfolk Tides (Baltimore Orioles)
17. Oklahoma City Dodgers (Los Angeles Dodgers)
18. Omaha Storm Chasers (Kansas City Royals)
19. Reno Aces (Arizona Diamondbacks)
20. Rochester Red Wings (Washington Nationals)
21. Round Rock Express (Texas Rangers)
22. Sacramento River Cats (San Francisco Giants)
23. Salt Lake Bees (Los Angeles Angels)
24. Scranton/Wilkes-Barre RailRiders (New York Yankees)
25. St. Paul Saints (Minnesota Twins)
26. Sugarland Skeeters (Houston Astros)
27. Syracuse Mets (New York Mets)
28. Tacoma Rainiers (Seattle Mariners)
29. Toledo Mud Hens (Detroit Tigers)
30. Worcester Red Sox (Boston Red Sox)

Double A Teams

The following are Double A teams in the MiLB:

1. Akron RubberDucks (Cleveland Indians)
2. Altoona Curve (Pittsburgh Pirates)

3. Amarillo Sod Poodles (Arizona Diamondbacks)
4. Arkansas Travelers (Seattle Mariners)
5. Birmingham Barons (Chicago White Sox)
6. Biloxi Shuckers (Milwaukee Brewers)
7. Birmingham Rumble Ponies (New York Mets)
8. Bowie Baysox (Baltimore Orioles)
9. Chattanooga Lookouts (Cincinnati Reds)
10. Corpus Christi Hooks (Houston Astros)
11. Erie SeaWolves (Detroit Tigers)
12. Frisco RoughRiders (Texas Rangers)
13. Hartford Yard Goats (Colorado Rockies)
14. Harrisburg Senators (Washington Nationals)
15. Midland RockHands (Oakland Athletics)
16. Mississippi Braves (Atlanta Braves)
17. Montgomery Biscuits (Tampa Bag Rays)
18. New Hampshire Fisher Cats (Toronto Blue Jays)
19. Northwest Arkansas Naturals (Kansas City Royals)
20. Pensacola Blue Wahoos (Miami Marlins)
21. Portland Sea Dogs (Boston Red Sox)
22. Reading Fightin Phils (Philadelphia Phillies)
23. Richmond Flying Squirrels (San Francisco Giants)
24. Rocket City Trash Pandas (Los Angeles Angels)
25. San Antonio Missions (San Diego Padres)
26. Somerset Patriots (New York Yankees)
27. Springfield Cardinals (St. Louis Cardinals)

28. Tennessee Smokies (Chicago Cubs)
29. Tulsa Drillers (Los Angeles)
30. Wichita Wind Surge (Minnesota Twins)

Class A Advanced (High A)

This is a list of the Class A Advanced Minor League teams and the MLB teams with which they are affiliated:

1. Aberdeen Ironbirds (Baltimore Orioles)
2. Asheville Tourists (Houston Astros)
3. Beloit Sky Carp (Miami Marlins)
4. Bowling Green Hot Rods (Tampa Bay Rays)
5. Brooklyn Cyclones (New York Mets)
6. Cedar Rapids Kernels (Minnesota Twins)
7. Dayton Dragons (Cincinnati Reds)
8. Eugene Emeralds (San Francisco Giants)
9. Everett AquaSox (Seattle Mariners)
10. Fort Wayne TinCaps (San Diego Padres)
11. Great Lakes Loons (Los Angeles Dodgers)
12. Greensboro Grasshoppers (Pittsburgh Pirates)
13. Greenville Drive (Boston Red Sox)
14. Hickory Crawdads (Texas Rangers)
15. Hillsboro Hops (Arizona Diamondbacks)
16. Hudson Valley Renegades (New York Yankees)
17. Jersey Shore Blue Claws (Philadelphia Phillies)
18. Lake County Captains (Cleveland Indians)
19. Lansing Lugnuts
20. Peoria Chiefs (St. Louis Cardinals)

21. Quad Cities River Bandits (Kansas City Royals)
22. Rome Braves (Atlanta Braves)
23. South Bend Cubs (Chicago Cubs)
24. Spokane Indians (Colorado Rockies)
25. Tri City Dust Devils (Los Angeles Angels)
26. Vancouver Cardinals (Toronto Blue Jays)
27. West Michigan Whitecaps (Detroit Tigers)
28. Wilmington Blue Rocks (Washington Nationals)
29. Winston-Salem Dash (Chicago White Sox)
30. Wisconsin Timber Rattlers (Milwaukee Brewers)

Class A (Low A)

This is a list of the Class A teams in Minor League baseball and the teams with which they are affiliated:

1. Augusta Green Jackets (Atlanta Braves)
2. Bradenton Marauders (Pittsburgh Pirates)
3. Carolina Mudcats (Milwaukee Brewers)
4. Charleston RiverDogs (Tampa Bay Rays)
5. Columbia Fireflies (Kansas City Royals)
6. Clearwater Threshers (Philadelphia Phillies)
7. Daytona Tortugas (Cincinnati Reds)
8. Delmarva Shorebirds (Baltimore Orioles)
9. Down East Wood Ducks (Texas Rangers)
10. Dunedin Blue Jays (Toronto Blue Jays)
11. Fayetteville Woodpeckers (Houston Astros)
12. Fort Myers Mighty Mussels (Minnesota Twins)

13. Fredericksburg Nationals (Washington Nationals)
14. Fresno Grizzlies (Colorado Rockies)
15. Inland Empire 66ers (Los Angeles Angels)
16. Jupiter Hammerheads (Miami Marlins)
17. Kannapolis Cannon Ballers (Chicago White Sox)
18. Lake Elsinore Storm (San Diego Padres)
19. Lakeland Flying Tigers (Detroit Tigers)
20. Lynchburg Hillcats (Cleveland Indians)
21. Modesto Nuts (Seattle Mariners)
22. Myrtle Beach Pelicans (Chicago Cubs)
23. Palm Beach Cardinals (St. Louis Cardinals)
24. Salem Red Sox (Boston Red Sox)
25. Rancho Cucamonga Quakes (Los Angeles Dodgers)
26. San Jose Giants (San Francisco Giants)
27. St. Lucie Mets (New York Mets)
28. Stockton Ports (Oakland Athletics)
29. Tampa Tarpons (New York Yankees)
30. Visalia Rawhide (Arizona Diamondbacks)

Class A Short Season (Short Season)

This is a list of the Short Season MiLB teams. As of 2021, the MiLB has actually reorganized the leagues and done away with the Short Season Leagues. However, here is the list of former teams. Some of these teams, you will notice, are on the list above. That is because a few of the Short Season teams were reorganized into the Class A League.

1. Aberdeen IronBirds
2. Auburn Doubledays
3. Batavia Muckdogs
4. Boise Hawks
5. Brooklyn Cyclones
6. Connecticut Tigers
7. Eugene Emeralds
8. Everett AquaSox
9. Hillsboro Hops
10. Hudson Valley Renegades
11. Lowell Spinners
12. Mahoning Valley Scrappers
13. Norwich Sea Unicorns
14. Salem-Keizer Volcanoes
15. Spokane Indians
16. State College Spikes
17. Staten Island Yankees
18. Tri-City Dust Devils
19. TriCity ValleyCats
20. Vermont Lake Monsters
21. West Virginia Black Bears
22. Williamsport Crosscutters
23. Vancouver Canadians

Rookie Teams

The rookie teams are split into three different leagues: The Arizona Complex League, the Florida Complex League, and the Dominican Summer League. The three leagues have 17, 19, and 46 teams, respectively.

Top 10 Minor League Teams

This list is the top 10 ranked Minor League teams as of 2021, based on their roster (list of players) and their season success (Glaser, 2021).

1. *Durham Bulls*: The Durham Bulls are a Triple A team affiliated with the Tampa Bay Rays. They had a successful season and also drafted nine of the top 30 prospects (most promising players) for this year.

2. *New Hampshire Fisher Cats*: The Fisher Cats are a Double A team affiliated with the Toronto Blue Jays. They had a great season and drafted five of the top 30 prospects in the Minor League.

3. *Everett AquaSox*: The AquaSox are a High-A team that hosts ten of the top 30 prospects and three of the Top 100 prospects in the MiLB. They are affiliated with the Seattle Mariners.

4. *Pensacola Blue Wahoos*: The Wahoos are affiliated with the Miami Marlins and they are a Double A team. They host six of the top 30 prospects and two of the Top 100.

5. *Greensboro Grasshoppers*: The Grasshoppers are a High A team. They drafted six of the top 30 prospects and three of the top 100. They are affiliated with the Pittsburgh Pirates.

6. *San Jose Giants*: This team has a collection of eight of the top 30 prospects and two of the top 100. They are a Low-A team affiliated with the San Francisco Giants.

7. *Worcester Red Sox*: With seven top 30 players and two top 100 players, this Triple A team for the Boston Red Sox has a promising roster. A few of their players are expected to make the jump to the Major League next season.

8. *Bowie BaySox*: This team hosts four top 30 players and two top 100 players. They are a Double A team affiliated with the Baltimore Orioles.

9. *Brooklyn Cyclones*: This High A team is affiliated with the New York Mets. They host six top 30 players and two of the top 100 prospects. Two of their Pitchers are expected to move up in the near future.

10. *Tacoma Rainiers*: This team is the Triple A team for the Seattle Mariners. They have three top 30 and two top 100 prospects on their roster. They have quite a few players who are expected to move up in the future.

Top 12 Minor League Players

This is a list of the 12 best players currently playing for the Minor Leagues, as of the 2021 season (Aho, 2021).

- *Nate Pearson*: Right-handed Pitcher Pearson has played for the Toronto Blue Jays (MLB) but he is recovering from an injury, so he is currently playing in the Triple A league in Buffalo to make sure he is ready to rejoin the Major Leagues.

- *Spencer Howard*: Howard is considered the Phillies' top prospect Pitcher. He is a right-handed Pitcher getting ready to move up to the Major League..

- *Delvi Garcia*: This right-handed Pitcher started with 33 strikeouts in his 2019 season. He is expected to move from the Triple A League to the Yankees soon.

- *Josiah Gray*: This right-handed Pitcher had a successful season this year, and is expected to move up to Triple A next year. His team is affiliated with the Los Angeles Dodgers.

- *Jose Garcia*: Many call Garcia the Reds' future Shortstop, but there's the fact that the Reds already need one. So, hopefully Garcia will move up to the Major Leagues soon.

- *Matthew Liberatore*: This left-handed Pitcher is expected to make the jump from the Redbirds to the Cardinals this year.

- *Nolan Jones*: This Third Baseman had a great season and is the top prospect for the Indians' next season.

- *Adley Rutschman*: This Catcher has had a great season and is all but a member of the Baltimore Orioles.

- *Brett Baty*: This player was chosen in the first round of the draft and is crossing his fingers that he will join the New York Mets soon).

- *Shea Langliers*: This 23-year-old catcher has been incredibly successful this season and is thought to be moving up to the Atlanta Braves next year.

- *Daniel Lynch*: This 24-year-old left-handed pitcher has actually been in the Majors with the Kansas City Royals, but he had to take a step down to Triple A due to an injury.

- *Marco Luciano*: This Shortstop from the Dominican Republic is expected to sign a million-dollar deal with the San Francisco Giants in the near future.

Summary

Wow! That's a lot of teams. With the end of the Short Season leagues, this should lead to players making it through the tiers and into the Major Leagues faster than in previous years. Maybe that list of 23 players who skipped the Minor Leagues will grow in the next few years!

If you live in one of the cities where a MiLB team plays, don't hesitate to go to a game! Minor League baseball can be incredibly entertaining, seats are often less expensive than MLB tickets, and how cool would it be to tell your friends in a few years that their favorite MLB player hit a Home Run in your hometown before he was famous?

Chapter 10
World Series History

We've talked a lot about baseball history. We've mentioned teams who won several World Series titles, and the coaches who joined them in their victory. It is the most important part of the season, the goal that every team in both leagues strive for. The Series winner is whoever gets the best of seven games. In other words, the team who wins four of the seven games is declared the champion.

But what are the coolest parts of the World Series? Here is a list of the top 15 moments in World Series history according to FoxSports (2016).

Fifteen World Series Moments to Remember

#15. 2001: Diamondbacks vs. Yankees, Game Four

The Yankees were losing, with the Diamondbacks winning two games and losing one. This fourth game was looking bad for the Yankees, as the Diamondbacks were winning 3-1. But then, batter Tino Ramirez hit a

Home Run that resulted in two points being scored in the bottom of the ninth inning, tying the score and leading to extra innings. The next inning had Derek Jeter hitting the game winning Home Run and giving the Yankees a renewed hope of winning the Series. Sadly, they went on to lose to the Diamondbacks anyway, but this particular game was one for the books.

#14. 1932: Yankees vs. the Cubs, Game Three

This game was a legend. Cubs fans and players had apparently been teasing Babe Ruth the entire game, giving Ruth a bit of a big head. This led to him "calling his shot." He came up to the plate to bat and took four pitches from Charlie Root. He had two strikes and two balls when he pointed his wooden bat deep into centerfield, and then assumed his batting stance. The next pitch Root threw, Ruth smacked the ball right over the centerfield wall-right where he pointed, his second Home Run of the game. Many people say he didn't actually point out his shot, that he was just trying to annoy Cubs fans and players. Some say he was pointing at Root, not calling his shot. But no matter what, Ruth's homer went down in World Series history. The Yankees went on to win the game and the Series.

#13. 1985: Cardinals vs. Royals, Game Six

The Cardinals were about to win the game—and the Series—when something terrible happened. A ground ball was hit to First Base and the umpire made a terrible call. Royals player Jorge Orta hit the ball, but he did not make it to First before Cardinals First Baseman Todd Worrell tagged the base. However, umpire Don Denkinger called Orta as safe, letting him remain on First. Many think this was the worst call in history, and this led to the Royals scoring two points and winning the game, then they beat the Cardinals in Game 7.

#12. 1997: Marlins vs. Indians, Game Seven

It was the last game in the Series. The winner of this one would be crowned champion. It was the bottom of the ninth inning, and the score was tied after Craig Counsell hit a ball that resulted in an RBI. In the 11th inning, Edgar Renteria came up to bat. The bases were loaded. There were two outs, so Renteria needed a hit. And then, he got one. He hit a single that resulted in Counsell making it Home and scoring. They won the game and the Series.

#11. 1956: Dodgers vs. Yankees, Game Five

Pitcher Don Larsen started this game, his second start of the Series. His first start in game two ended in two innings after four runs were scored with him on the mound. He had better luck this time, retiring all 27 of the Dodgers batters, including Dick Williams, Jackie Robinson, Pee Wee Reese, Roy Campanella, and Duke Snyder, all future Hall of Famers at the time. This was the first and only perfect game in World Series history.

The Yankees won the game 2–0 and won the Series in seven games.

#10. 2011: Cardinals vs. Rangers, Game Six

The Rangers were winning the Series with a 3–2 lead. The Rangers only had to win one more to be the champions. In game six, the Cardinals were losing 7–5 in the bottom of the ninth inning. Then, Rangers Pitcher Neftali Feliz came to close the game. Albert Pujols hit a double off of him, and Feliz walked Lance Berkman. There were two outs when David Freese tied the game with a triple, knocking in two RBIs and sending the game into extra innings. The game was still tied in the 11th inning when Freese came to bat again, hitting a game winning Home Run with a second game-saving hit. The Cardinals would go on to game seven and win the Series.

#9. 2001: Diamondbacks vs. Yankees, Game Seven

Arizona was losing the game 2–1 when they entered the final inning of the last game. Pitcher Mariano Rivera took the mound to close the game for the Yankees, and things weren't looking good for the Diamondbacks. Then, Mark Grace hit a single, followed by Tony Womack hitting a double and an RBI that tied the game. Finally, Luis Gonzales, who had hit 57 Home Runs that season, stepped up to the plate. The following hit led to the game winning run, and the Diamondbacks won the Series.

#8. 1954: Giants vs. Indians, Game One

This game was tied 2–2 in the eighth inning. There was a runner on First and another on Second when Indians batter, Vic Wertz, came to the plate. Wertz was already responsible for the two points the Indians had, and then he hit another long hit. He took off running, ready to score, when Willie Mays took off in a dead sprint and caught the ball, one of the most famous catches in baseball history. It's known as "The Catch." Wertz was out, and the Giants went on to win the game and the Series.

#7. 1991: Twins vs Braves, Game Six

This Series is considered to be one of the greatest in baseball history. Five of the seven games were decided by a team's last at-bat. This game was one of them. In the 11th inning, the score was tied 3–3 when Kirby Puckett hit a Home Run into center field and won the game. The Twins went on to win the Series in game seven.

#6. 1986: Mets vs. Red Sox, Game Six

The Red Sox had not won a Series in 68 years, and they were itching to break that streak. They were winning by two in the bottom of the ninth inning of this game with two outs. Then, Mets batter Mookie Wilson hit a ground ball that went right to First Baseman Bill Buckner. Right before Buckner caught the easy hit and got the last out for the Sox, the ball bounced a weird way and headed straight for right field. The mistake led to the Mets winning the game and then the Series in game seven.

#5. 1975: Reds vs. Red Sox, Game Six

This is called one of the greatest games in baseball history. The Red Sox were down 3–2 in the Series and were losing game six 6–3 in the bottom of the eighth. Bernie Carbo came up to bat and tied the game with a Home Run. In the bottom of the 12th inning, Carlton Fisk came to the plate. He hit a ball wide left, heading towards foul territory. He started waving his hands towards fair territory as if he could push the ball in the air. It worked. The ball remained in fair territory and earned Fisk a Home Run that won the Sox the game. Sadly, the Reds beat them in game seven and won the Series.

#4. 1977: Yankees vs. Dodgers, Game Six

The Yankees were winning the Series with a 3–2 win. Reggie Jackson was thriving in game six after hitting two Home Runs in the previous two games. In game six, he hit three Home Runs. The only other player at the time to have hit three Home Runs in a World Series was Babe Ruth. Jackson's five homers tied a record also set by Ruth. Jackson earned the nickname 'Mr. October,' and the Yankees won their first Series since 1962.

#3. 1988: Dodgers vs. Athletics, Game One

When injured Dodgers player Kirk Gibson came up to bat as pinch hitter at the bottom of the ninth inning, fans were shocked. The Dodgers were down 4–3, and the Athletics closer Dennis Eckersley was the American League's best closing Pitcher that year. There was a runner on base after A's Pitcher Eckersley got two quick outs. Then, Gibson limped to the plate. He had two strikes and three balls, something called a *full count*. Then, he hit a ball into right field that tied the game. The Dodgers went on to win the game and the Series, but Gibson did not play again for the rest of the Series.

#2. 1993: Blue Jays vs. Phillies, Game Six

The Blue Jays were winning the Series with a 3–2 lead, but this game wasn't going well for them after the Phillies scored six runs, leading 6–5. Phillies closer Mitch "Wild Thing" Williams took the mound, but walked Rickey Henderson and gave up a single to Paul Molitor. Joe Carter came to the plate then, hitting two strikes and two balls. Then, he finally hit the ball right over the left field wall, right out of the park, and won the Series for the Blue Jays for the second time in 2 years.

#1. 1960: Pirates vs. Yankees, Game Seven

The Pirates were winning this game 9–7 after they scored five runs in the eighth inning, but the ninth inning saw the Yankees tie the score. Then, Pirates Second Baseman Bill Mazeroski came to bat, hitting a homer right over left field. The Pirates won the game and the Series, 10–9. It was the first Series-winning Home Run in baseball history.

Summary

The World Series is something baseball fans look forward to from the end of game seven until the following October. Historic moments like this are the kind that bring fans out of their seats, both at home and at the stadium, with their arms up in the air as they cheer. These jaw dropping occurrences are what keep people coming back for more when it comes to baseball, and history is being made every day.

Chapter 11
Twenty-Five Best Baseball Movies

If you have friends that are baseball fans, they likely have a favorite baseball movie. There are animated movies, documentaries, historical fiction pictures, and even legacy films based on real stories. There are tons of movies about baseball and the players, teams, and coaches. Here are 25 great ones. This list is based on how well the movies represent the game of baseball, as well as the quality of the individual movies, according to Will Leitch (2021).

#1. Bull Durham (1988)

Bull Durham is about the Single A team, the Durham Bulls. They are having a poorly attended season, but they have a very promising Pitcher: Calvin LaLoosh. Then, 12-year MLB Catcher Crash Davis is sent to the Minor Leagues to help turn LaLoosh into an MLB Pitcher. This movie has an all star cast, including Susan Sarandon and Kevin Costner. It speaks on the importance of encouraging teammates and motivational coaching.

#2. A League of Their Own (1992)

This movie is about the true story of the All American Girls Professional Baseball League that formed during World War II. A team of women deals with the struggles and difficulties that come with a woman playing professional baseball at the time. But the women want to be great baseball players, and Tom Hanks plays a manager who's willing to take them there. He believes in them when they need him to and encourages them to be tough and strong ("There's no crying in baseball!"). This movie is inspiring and emotional, also starring none other than Madonna and Geena Davis. It's a must-see.

#3. The Pride of the Yankees (1942)

This movie is a tear-jerker. It tells the story of Lou Gehrig and his struggle with ALS, later nicknamed "Lou Gehrig's disease." The actor who portrayed Gehrig was Gary Cooper, who many say looked just like the player himself. There is also a jaw-dropping portrayal of Babe Ruth … played by Babe Ruth!

#4. Field of Dreams (1989)

This movie is about a troubled farmer with a poor relationship with his now-dead father, who hears a voice in his dream. The voice says, "If you build it, he will come." The farmer builds a baseball field on his land, and the ghosts of famous baseball players come out to play the game, including Shoeless Joe Jackson (a legendary outfielder for the Chicago White Sox whose career was cut short after being caught up in a scandal, portrayed in movie #5, *Eight Men Out*). After a whirlwind of events, the farmer realizes that of all the ghosts on his field, he wishes his father was one of them. This movie also stars Kevin Costner, Burt Lancaster, and James Earl Jones and is based on the book *Shoeless Joe* by W. P, Kinsella.

#5. Eight Men Out (1988)

The Chicago White Sox suffered a terrible scandal in 1919. Called the 'Black Sox Scandal,' this incident involved eight players (including legendary outfielder Shoeless Joe Jackson, so named for having played a game in his socks when the shoes he was wearing were too uncomfortable) who were accused of purposely losing the World Series in exchange for money from a gambler. The players were banned from Major League baseball and excluded from being considered for the Hall of Fame. This movie is a historical picture about that story.

#6. Moneyball (2011)

Starring dynamic duo Jonah Hill and Brad Pitt, this movie is about the math and data collection that occurs in baseball. It shows the true story of how Athletics manager Billy Beane made the As a great team on a low budget by trading and drafting players that other teams overlooked. It introduces a whole new look to the sport, based on the book by the same name by Michael Lewis.

#7. The Natural (1984)

This romance movie was actually based on a novel of the same name by Bernard Malamud. This is the story of a man on his way to try out for the Chicago Cubs when he is seriously injured. Sixteen years later, he returns to play for a rookie team in last place. He decides to put in a lot of work to turn the team around, to the disappointment of the team's owner. The book ends with Hobbs, the main character played by Robert Redford, giving up and purposely losing a game to please the owner, letting down his team and his fans. However, the director decided to change the ending to the movie, making it a little less heartbreaking in the end.

#8. The Sandlot (1993)

"You're killin' me Smalls!" Have you ever heard this phrase? It came from this movie, which is about a little boy who knows nothing about baseball, then moves to a new town and meets some new friends who play on a dirt field in their neighborhood (the sandlot). It's a great movie to watch, lots of fun-and a lot of history about Babe Ruth.

#9. Major League (1989)

This is one of those movies that every baseball player loves. When a new owner Rachel Phelps gets a deal to move the Cleveland Indians to Miami, she has to do some quick plotting. She hires some incompetent players in order to make ticket sales plummet so she can break her contract to move the team. However, she accidentally puts together an inspiring team that manages to steal the hearts of fans in Cleveland. It stars well known stars Charlie Sheen and Tom Berenger.

#10. The Bad News Bears (1976)

This is a movie about a disgraced former Minor League player (played by Walter Matthau) who agrees to coach a Little League (kids) team. The team he is assigned is the worst in the league, but this coach has a plan to whip them into shape.

#11. Bang the Drum Slowly (1973)

Another tear jerker, this movie is about a mentally handicapped catcher who contracts a terminal illness. People bully him, but he makes friends with a good hearted pitcher. This movie stars Robert De Niro.

#12. The Bingo Long Traveling All-Stars and Motor Kings (1976)

This is a period piece about the segregated leagues and the stars who joined a travel team in the 1930s. The team took the world by storm and inspired many. It stars many well known actors, including the legendary James Earl Jones.

#13. The Rookie (2002)

This is an underdog story about Jim Morris, a high school science teacher who made the Major League at the late age of 35 years old .

#14. Take Me Out To the Ball Game

This one is actually a musical! Two key players for a team called the Wolves, Dennis Ryan and Eddie O'Brien, have a passion for theater. A gambler bets on the Wolves to lose a game and wants to get their star player off the field, so he offers O'Brien a place in a new theater production. O'Brien wants to, but he doesn't want to let his team down. This movie stars Frank Sinatra and Gene Kelly.

#15. Da*n Yankees (1958)

This musical is about a fan who loves the Nationals so much that he literally makes a deal with the devil so the team can beat the Yankees. The Yankees are still called that to this day.

#16. Sugar (2008)

Another under-appreciated movie, this independent film is about a Dominican Republic player who struggles to survive and acclimate to the Minor Leagues when he comes to America.

#17. Fear Strikes Out (1957)

This movie was revolutionary for its time when it portrayed Red Sox player Jimmy Piershall's struggle with mental illness. He was played by Anthony Perkins.

#18. 42 (2013)

This movie is about Jackie Robinson (played by Chadwick Boseman) and Branch Rickey's (played by Harrison Ford) efforts to desegregate baseball. See Chapter 3 for more of a discussion of Jackie Robinson.

#19. Rookie of the Year (1993)

This kids movie is about a fan in the stands who's favorite team, the Chicago Cubs, picks him from the stands and lets him pitch for them. It's every child's dream!

#20. Angels in the Outfield (1994)

When a little boy asks his dad if his family will ever be together again, his dad tells him that it'll only happen when the Anaheim Angels win the World Series. Considering the Angels are the worst team in the MLB, the little boy starts praying. Then, a real angel decides to help the boy out… and the Angels start winning.

#21. 61 (2001)

This movie is about the Home Run race that took place between Mickey Mantle and Roger Maris. It's quite thrilling to watch.

#22. Cobb (1994)

This movie is about Ty Cobb in his earliest years of baseball. While we know more about Cobb now than we did then, this movie portrays Cobb to be a cruel and rude player, although he was one of the best baseball players of all time.

#23. For the Love of the Game (1999)

Kevin Costner stars in yet another movie on our list. He plays a pitcher at the end of his career who wants to retire on a good note. He is struggling with that goal and his relationship, but with his team, he might have a chance

#24. Fever Pitch (2005)

This romance is about a couple who don't have much in common but fall in love anyway. Then, the woman realizes that her new boyfriend is absolutely obsessed with the Boston Red Sox, to the point where she feels like she's competing with the whole team. It's a fun movie starring Jimmy Fallon and Drew Barrymore.

#25. Million Dollar Arm (2014)

This is a story about a sports agent who's desperate to save his career. He travels to India to find a cricket player he thinks he can turn into a Major League star.

Honorable Mentions

The previous list are 25 great movies, but they're certainly not all of them. Here are a few movies you also shouldn't miss.

1. *Everyone's Hero* (2006)
2. *Hardball* (2001)
3. *Air Bud* (1997)
4. *A Mile in His Shoes* (2011)
5. *The Jackie Robinson Story* (1950)

Ken Burns also did a very good nine-part documentary on the history of baseball, titled *Baseball*.

Conclusion

We made it! Now, I hope you know the basic rules of baseball and how to play, so you can join your friends in the next backyard game they play. That way, when someone asks if you want to play Second Base or Left Field, you know where to go and hopefully have an idea of how to play it. You know the various pitches and where on the bat to hit the ball. You know where the bases are and what to do to avoid being tagged out. You also know the strike zone and the proper equipment to be worn by the players.

Then there were all those rules about fielding and batting and running and uniforms. Can you remember them all? Don't worry if you can't, that's what the umpires are for. They keep the game fair and make decisions so the players don't have to.

You also learned a lot about the history of baseball. We talked about where it came from, how it started, the games that inspired it, and the people responsible for turning it into the game it is today. We also talked about a lot of the myths surrounding the creation of baseball and how the game has changed over time. We discussed the importance of regulating the weight of the actual baseball, the length and weight of the bat, why teams have shortened outfields, and why the position of the Designated Hitter was invented. Then, we discussed how technology has made the game more fair and more exciting.

Once we talked about those positions, you learned the players who made the positions shine during their careers. You learned why Catcher is arguably the most difficult position, and why the game depends so heavily on the pitcher. We learned a lot about players who didn't only make their positions well known, but became the face of baseball for their time. We learned *why* Babe Ruth is so well known, as well as talked about some of the more recent famous players.

We talked about the best teams and why they were so noteworthy. What made those teams special, and why have they gone down in history? When were they at their peak performance? What players were on those teams that made history?

We also talked about the managers that led those teams to make history. Between amazing players and fantastic coaches, some of these teams were an unstoppable force on the baseball field. Who made it into the Hall of Fame, and why?

And then we learned about the coolest records and some super interesting facts about the sport. Who knew a simple game could last so long? Can you imagine playing baseball for eight hours straight, like they did in 1984? I would certainly be ready for a meal and some sleep by the end of that!

Once we knew the basics of baseball, we talked about how baseball has expanded to countries all over the world, and the places that have the largest baseball following besides the United States.

We then went into the Major League teams that play today. Which ones are in the National League? What about the American League? How many teams are there? What about the fields they play on? What are the names of the stadiums? Baseball fans often look forward to getting to attend the stadium and see the field of their favorite team in person. Many fans dream of walking on those fields themselves.

Then there's the Minor League. What is it, and why is it important? How many teams are there, and who are they? We talked about the tiers and what they're there for. We discussed the Short Season before it was dissolved in 2021, and the teams that were a part of it before its demise. Finally, we discussed the teams in each tier of the MiLB and which MLB team they are affiliated with. We listed the top 10 players that played in the Minor Leagues in 2021 and who they played for.

Then, we discussed the World Series. These two important words are littered throughout the book, sure, but why? What are some of the coolest moments that have taken place in the World Series? Why were they significant? Who was responsible for creating this history? We talked about the reason fans look forward to these championships and why every team hopes to play in them.

Then we went on to learn about the greatest baseball movies. Movies like *A League of Their Own*, *Field of Dreams*, and *Pride of the Yankees* are timeless classics that everyone should see at least once in their lifetime. We discussed fans' love of these movies and why, and the inspiration behind them. Of course, if those aren't the movies for you, you can also find joy in watching movies such as *42*, *Everyone's Hero*, or *Heading Home*.

It's a lot of fun to go to a baseball game at a stadium. There's nothing quite like singing "Take Me Out to the Ballgame" with thousands of other fans, eating a delicious hot dog while your favorite player hits a Home Run, making the crowd go wild, and participating in the Seventh Inning Stretch after sitting still for a tad too long. Not to mention getting to brag to your friends about how you were there when your favorite Major League player hit his first ever Home Run when he played in the Double A League, or when you got to see a Pitcher throw a no-hitter for the first time.

I hope this book has given you as much love for the sport as I have. Being a part of baseball is so much fun. There are so many inspiring players and stories that you can learn a lot from, I know I sure did! And if you aren't officially a baseball fan, that's okay too, but I sure hope you learned something during our journey together!

Now that you've learned all there is to know (for now), go take these new tools and use them!

DISCUSSION

This section is a short quiz to help you remember what you've learned. No pressure! Just a quick guide to baseball, in case you need a refresher. The answers are located at the end of the questions. Remember, you can always look back at what we've talked about if you're not sure of the answer.

1. How many positions are there on a baseball field?
    a. Three
    b. Ten
    c. Nine
    d. Seven
2. What is the other name for the coach in Major League Baseball?
    a. Manager
    b. Owner
    c. Boss
    d. None of the above

3. What is the name of the player who tries to hit the ball thrown by the pitcher?
    a. Catcher
    b. Batter
    c. Swinger
    d. Runner
4. What is a Home Run?
    a. When the player runs to the edge of the field
    b. When the ball is hit out of the field (Park)
    c. When the player hits the ball and crosses all four bases in one run
    d. When the pitcher throws three strikes at the batter
5. Which team has the most members in the Hall of Fame?
    a. Boston Red Sox
    b. St. Louis Cardinals
    c. Baltimore Orioles
    d. New York Yankees
6. Which team is the oldest in baseball?
    a. Boston Red Sox
    b. Atlanta Braves
    c. Washington Nationals
    d. New York Yankees
7. Which player holds the record for the most games played in a row?
    a. Babe Ruth
    b. Lou Gehrig

    c. Cal Ripken Jr.

    d. David Ortiz

8. Which of these records is considered 'unbreakable'?

    a. Joe DiMaggio's Hit Streak

    b. Ty Cobb's batting average

    c. Nolan Ryan's career strikeouts

    d. All of the above

9. Which team did Babe Ruth play for before he was traded to the Yankees?

    a. St. Louis Cardinals

    b. Boston Red Sox

    c. Chicago Cubs

    d. Cincinnati Reds

10. Who was credited with inventing baseball, but actually had nothing to do with it?

    a. Babe Ruth

    b. Rollie Fingers

    c. Abner Doubleday

    d. Abner Graves

11. Even though the Braves are the oldest MLB team, which team was the first openly professional team?

    a. Chicago Cubs

    b. Cincinnati Red Stockings

    c. New York Yankees

    d. Washington Senators

12. Which player holds the record for stolen bases?
    a. Babe Ruth
    b. Lou Gehrig
    c. Rickey Henderson
    d. Albert Pujols
13. Which player has a record holding 56 game hitting streak?
    a. Babe Ruth
    b. Joe DiMaggio
    c. Lou Gehrig
    d. David Ortiz
14. Which manager has the record for the most games won in a career?
    a. Connie Mack
    b. Tony LaRussa
    c. Bobby Cox
    d. Earl Weaver
15. In what year did the Boston Red Sox win the World Series and break the "Curse of the Bambino?"
    a. 2000
    b. 2001
    c. 2002
    d. 2004
16. Which of these managers won seven World Series Titles?
    a. Joe Torre
    b. Joe McCarthy
    c. Earl Weaver

      d. Bobby Cox
17. What is the Minor League?
    a. Professional League before Major League
    b. Recreational League
    c. College League
    d. High School League
18. How many tiers are in the MiLB?
    a. Two
    b. Three
    c. Five
    d. Six
19. What is the highest tier in Minor League baseball?
    a. Double A
    b. High A
    c. Triple A
    d. Short Season
20. How many teams are in the Major League?
    a. 10
    b. 20
    c. 30
    d. 40
21. How many teams are in the National League?
    a. 10
    b. 15
    c. 20
    d. 30

22. Which of these teams is not located in the United States?
    a. Rays
    b. Blue Jays
    c. Astros
    d. Expos
23. How many Triple A teams are there?
    a. 25
    b. 30
    c. 50
    d. 75
24. In what year did Babe Ruth famously "call his shot" during the World Series?
    a. 1920
    b. 1932
    c. 1940
    d. 1950
25. What team lost the World Series after a ground ball bounced past the First Baseman?
    a. New York Yankees
    b. Boston Red Sox
    c. Chicago Cubs
    d. Atlanta Braves
26. What team had the first World Series winning Home Run?
    a. Pirates
    b. Giants
    c. Cubs
    d. Yankees

27. What year did Carlton Fisk hit a ball and wave his arms until the ball was in fair territory?
    a. 1975
    b. 1985
    c. 1995
    d. 2005
28. Which of these movies is about women playing Major League Baseball?
    a. *Field of Dreams*
    b. *42*
    c. *A League of Their Own*
    d. *Major League*
29. Which of these movies tells the story of Lou Gehrig?
    a. *Pride of the Yankees*
    b. *61*
    c. *Field of Dreams*
    d. *Fear Strikes Out*
30. Which of these movies is about ghosts of former players playing baseball?
    a. *42*
    b. *61*
    c. *Major League*
    d. *Field of Dreams*

Answers

1. C
2. A
3. B
4. C
5. D
6. B
7. C
8. D
9. B
10. C
11. B
12. C
13. B
14. A
15. D
16. B
17. A
18. B
19. C
20. C
21. B
22. B
23. B
24. B
25. B
26. A
27. A
28. C
29. A
30. D

How did you do? I love using quizzes to test knowledge on your recent learning. And, if you need a quick refresher in the future when you're getting ready to watch or play some baseball, this quiz should help you find some quick facts!

just for you

A Free Gift For Our Readers
Please grab your FREE
Sports History Starter Guide for Kids
by clicking the link below!

REFERENCES

10 oldest baseball teams in America. (2017, December 2). Oldest.org. Retrieved November 14, 2021, https://www.oldest.org/sports/baseball-teams-america/

Aho, C. (2021). *Top players in Minor League Baseball.* Google. Retrieved November 19, 2021, https://www.google.com/amp/s/usa.inquirer.net/76700/top-players-in-minor-league-baseball/amp

All-american girls professional baseball league. (n.d.) Wikipedia. Retrieved November 20, 2021, https://en.m.wikipedia.org/wiki/All-American_Girls_Professional_Baseball_League.

Allen, N. I. (2020, August 4). *Top 30 managers in Major League Baseball history.* AthlonSports. Retrieved November 14, 2021, https://athlonsports.com/mlb/top-30-managers-major-league-baseball-history

Andreajn. (2021, November 11). *120 exciting baseball facts nobody tells you about.* Facts.net. Retrieved November 14, 2021, https://facts.net/lifestyle/sports/baseball-facts/

Anicetti, D. (2021, January 9). *Top 20 major league baseball teams of all-time.* Fueled by Sports. Retrieved November 14, 2021, https://www.fueledbysports.com/top-20-major-league-baseball-teams-of-all-time/

Baseball positions: All 9 fielding positions explained. (2020, February 3). Baseball Coaching Lab. Retrieved November 14, 2021, https://baseballcoachinglab.com/baseball-positions/

Baseball uniform rules. (2016) NFHS. https://www.nfhs.org/sports-resource-content/baseball-uniform-rules/

Bernier, S. (n.d.). *What is minor league baseball?* Pro Baseball Insider. Retrieved November 16, 2021, http://probaseballinsider.com/what-is-minor-league-baseball/

Bolender, D. (2017, October 3). *MLB: Who's the best all-time at each position?* Bleacher Report. Retrieved November 14, 2021, https://bleacherreport.com/articles/9524-MLB-MLB_Who_s_The_Best_All-Time_at_Each_Position_-140208

Emrey, M. (2018, May 8). *Top 5 most unbreakable baseball records.* Bleacher Report. Retrieved November 14, 2021, https://bleacherreport.com/articles/22006-top-5-most-unbreakable-baseball-records

Evolution of sport—Baseball. (2015, August 4). Blast. Retrieved November 14, 2021, from https://blastmotion.com/blog/evolution-of-sport-baseball/#gref

Foxsports. (2013, October 21). *Top 15 most memorable world series moments.* FOX Sports. Retrieved November 16, 2021, https://www.foxsports.com/mlb/gallery/top-15-most-memorable-moments-in-world-series-history-102113

Glaser , K. (2021, May 4). *The top 10 most talented minor league rosters on Opening Day.* Google. Retrieved November 19, 2021, https://www.google.com/amp/s/www.baseballamerica.com/stories/the-top-10-most-talented-minor-league-rosters-on-opening-day/%3famphtml

High A. (n.d.). Wikipedia. Retrieved November 16, 2021, https://en.m.wikipedia.org/wiki/High-A

How to play baseball. (n.d.). Rules of Sport. Retrieved November 14, 2021, https://www.rulesofsport.com/sports/baseball.html

Leitch , W. (2021, August 11). *25 of the best baseball movies ever.* Google. Retrieved November 19, 2021, from https://www.google.com/amp/s/www.mlb.com/

amp/news/best-baseball-movies-of-all-time-c301609142.html?client=safari

List of Major League baseball managers by wins. (n.d.). Wikipedia. Retrieved November 14, 2021, https://en.wikipedia.org/wiki/List_of_Major_League_Baseball_managers_by_wins

List of Minor League baseball leagues and teams. (n.d.). Wikipedia. Retrieved November 16, 2021, https://en.m.wikipedia.org/wiki/List_of_Minor_League_Baseball_leagues_and_teams

List of MLB teams & stadiums (n.d.). GeoJango Maps. Retrieved November 16, 2021, https://geojango.com/pages/list-of-mlb-teams

List of MLB teams in the American League. (n.d.). Fueled by Sports. Retrieved November 16, 2021, https://www.fueledbysports.com/list-of-mlb-teams-in-the-american-league/

List of MLB teams in the National League. Fueled by Sports. (2020, June 30). Retrieved November 16, 2021, from https://www.fueledbysports.com/list-of-mlb-teams-in-the-national-league/

Low-A East. (n.d.). Wikipedia. Retrieved November 16, 2021, https://en.m.wikipedia.org/wiki/Low-A_East

Negro League Baseball. Wikipedia. Retrieved November 20, 2021, https://en.m.wikipedia.org/wiki/Negro_league_baseball

New York-Penn League. (n.d.). Minor League Baseball Wiki. Retrieved November 16, 2021, https://minor-league-baseball.fandom.com/wiki/New_York-Penn_League

Northwest League. (n.d.). Minor League Baseball Wiki. Retrieved November 16, 2021, https://minor-league-baseball.fandom.com/wiki/Northwest_League

Pinto, G. (2017, October 3). *The best player in MLB history, position by position.* Bleacher Report. Retrieved November 14, 2021, https://bleacherreport.com/articles/873330-the-best-player-in-mlb-history-position-by-position

Pitch Smart: Guidelines. MLB.com. (n.d.). Retrieved November 20, 2021, from https://www.mlb.com/pitch-smart/pitching-guidelines.

Popularity of baseball around the world. (n.d.). Topend Sports, science, training and nutrition. Retrieved November 16, 2021, from https://www.topendsports.com/world/lists/popular-sport/sports/baseball.htm

Rader, B. G. (2021, August 31). *baseball*. Encyclopedia Britannica. https://www.britannica.com/sports/baseball

Reuter, J. (2019, October 22). *Bleacher Report's official rankings of the 50 greatest teams in MLB history*. Bleacher Report. Retrieved November 19, 2021, https://bleacherreport.com/articles/1995178-bleacher-reports-official-rankings-of-the-50-greatest-teams-in-mlb-history

Rookie Leagues. (n.d.). MiLB.com. Retrieved November 16, 2021, https://www.milb.com/about/rookie.

Scott, N. (2021, April 23). *The 50 greatest yogi berra quotes*. USA Today. Retrieved November 20, 2021, from https://ftw.usatoday.com/2019/03/the-50-greatest-yogi-berra-quotes.

Staff, the Score. (2017). *Ranking the greatest position players in baseball history: Nos. 20-1*. theScore.com. Retrieved November 19, 2021, https://www.thescore.com/mlb/news/1449159

Top 10 unbreakable baseball records. (2018, May 25). Bat Flips and Nerds. Retrieved November 14, 2021, https://batflipsandnerds.com/2018/05/25/top-10-unbreakable-baseball-records/

This day in history. (2009, November 16). National League of Baseball is founded. History.com. Retrieved November 14, 2021, https://www.history.com/this-day-in-history/national-league-of-baseball-is-founded

Triple-A (baseball). (n.d.). Wikipedia. Retrieved November 16, 2021, https://en.m.wikipedia.org/wiki/Triple-A_(baseball)

Who invented baseball? (2013, March 27). History.com. Retrieved November 14, 2021, from https://www.history.com/news/who-invented-baseball

All images sourced from unsplash, https://unsplash.com

www.ingramcontent.com/pod-product-compliance
Lightning Source LLC
Chambersburg PA
CBHW020906080526
44589CB00011B/471